The Results Equation

From Dream to Done in 5 Simple Steps

The Results Equation

From Dream to Done in 5 Simple Steps

Kellan Fluckiger

The Results Equation

From Dream to Done in 5 Simple Steps

Red Aussie Publishing
22424 S Ellsworth Loop Rd
Unit 898
Queen Creek, AZ 85142

Contact the Publisher:
RedAussiePublishing@gmail.com
www.RedAussiePublishing.com

Contact the Author:
www.KellanFluckiger.com

Editing and Cover Design by Joy Fluckiger

ISBN: 978-1-7328588-3-1

Table of Contents

Foreword

When I met Kellan 6 years ago, I was equal parts passion, frustration, and chaos. I was clumsily navigating a transition from being a physician and video game developer to coaching physicians. To say my stuff was messy is an understatement.

I came to Kellan with a loose understanding of a set of concepts around how to take my dream and turn it into reality. I knew my process was full of holes and misconceptions because I had patched it together from books I had read, email sequences I had subscribed to, blogs and YouTube… you get the picture.

My system did not inspire confidence or guarantee results. It didn't help clear my head or give me an effective way of measuring progress or communicating with my collaborators. To be honest, I'm not sure what my system did other than let me say I had a system.

The Results Equation was immediately impactful for me. It was the first time I got the sense that everything I knew about my project was right there captured and that I was really going to get it accomplished.

Over the years, through adopting the Results Equation (RE) and my one-on-one and group coaching with Kellan, I have gained increasing competence in the RE process. With that has come the ability to feel confident dreaming about new ideas and opportunities for the future, knowing I have a framework and process which adapts to my mind, keeps me organized and honest, and lets me know how I'm doing.

As you learn the Results Equation, do the exercises. Yes, even the sometimes uncomfortable deep soul-searching and the awkward work in the mirror. This is a process that lives up to its name. You will get results. You will grow to become the person to do what you once believed impossible for you. You will feel better about yourself and more powerful.

I'm grateful that I have had the opportunity to make the Results Equation the fundamental core of how I do things. I trust you'll find it changes things for you equally powerfully.

Mani Saint-Victor, MD
Physician, Musician, Hypnotist.
Washington DC
April 2019

Introduction

Doing things is the story of human existence. We discover what went on in times past by the evidence we uncover. Buildings left behind, writings found and translated. Stories and legends passed down through generations.

Future generations will learn about us the same way. Now, with digital media, they will know exactly who we were, what we did or didn't do and all the rest in ridiculous detail.

It's in our nature to want to build, discover and grow. Why do some people boldly press forward and go after lofty goals, while the majority seem content to float down the river?

Is there a process or system that can be used reliably and repeatedly to aid us in creating our vision? Is there a tool that helps not only with the methods of planning and execution but also with the vagaries of motivation and perseverance?

Yes. There are already many approaches to "getting things done." There are hundreds of books on methods for setting goals, prioritizing, staying motivated and completing projects.

Project management is a university degree. Many other courses and certificates teach some part of the achievement game. So, why another book on creating results?

Because we need more, things change, and methods evolve. Despite the plenitude of published material, there is a real shortage of systems that apply to *any* goal.

There is also very little that deals simultaneously with both planning and execution, while at the same time addressing motivation, flexibility, and perseverance.

The time has come for a different approach. An approach that deals with the hard and soft sides of the art and science of "getting it done." This art involves the nuances of human behavior, motivation, and leadership. It includes understanding trends and the winds of change which affect the human side of achievement.

The science involves the mechanisms, tools, and money needed to plan, track and finish a project. Countless efforts to do something have started and then failed because one of these concrete elements was missing.

Comprehensive and flexible planning is another critical element in getting things done. Analysis of strengths and weaknesses, accurate predictions of time required, and anticipation of obstacles all play a huge role in manifesting success.

Even with all the material and methods about the individual parts required to make things happen, there is not enough material about how these fit together as a connected whole, especially with the dramatic increase in entrepreneurship, solopreneurship and internet business facilitated by the web.

That's why I wrote this book. It's a new look at the process of getting things done. All projects, whether they are "soft" or "hard," big or small, have common characteristics.

This book is not a detailed analysis of project management methods. Nor is it a deep psychological dive into the human psyche. Instead, it is a holistic description of how these things work together and a model about how to make it work for you.

We need to answer fundamental questions like:

- How do we decide what to do?
- How do we get organized to make it happen?
- How do we cultivate personal leadership and power to finish a project?
- What are the overarching principles to make things happen?

In this book, creating a result means getting from point "A" to point "B." I call it the journey from "here to there." Every result you want to accomplish can be thought of in this way.

Wherever I am is the starting point of any journey. It is by definition "here." Wherever I want to be, with whatever conditions and completed items at a point in the future, is "there."

Walking the path from here to there is the process required to get your desired result. Figuring out how to do that will vary with the type of project you have in mind. However, the principles and process remain the same. That is the beauty and power of "The Results Equation™."

A construction project requires external materials, money, time, labor, city permits, public meetings, ground composition studies, and many other things depending on the location and size of the project.

Any result involving an internal change, such as the acquisition or termination of a habit, requires no city permits but is often far more difficult because it takes place in the murky chambers of the mind, instead of blueprints and on the ground.

A championship performance in a sporting event requires training, dedication, significant mental work and the kind of commitment that no one ever knows except the coach and the athlete.

Even so, all the steps in moving from "here to there," can be described in much the same way. There is a logic and consistency to the process of achieving any result that you desire.

The purpose of this book is to describe this process to you. It's to help you understand the elegant simplicity that underlies all great achievement.

I have written this book for three reasons:

- First, over my decades of executive and consulting work, I have led many seemingly "impossible" projects and stood at the epicenter of significant change. In the inner game, I have experienced massive personal changes of the most challenging kind. Depression, addictions, attempted suicide, a near-death experience and much more. I wrote this book to create a map about how I accomplished what I did and how I saw this common thread in every kind of achievement.

- Second, I want to express the powerful simplicity and fantastic truth of the process of creating results. I want to clear away the fog, demystify the amazing and show that results of any size are available to anyone if they follow the steps. That means the process is available for you to get anything you want.

- Third, as a coach, my mission is to help people do things they don't believe they can do. Creating the results equation, running workshops to prove its efficacy and then writing the book allows me to help more people discover, develop and deliver or manifest their divine nature and gifts. It will help you do what you think is impossible.

I am not saying this is the only way to think about change and achieve results. I am not saying that other books and methods don't work.

I am saying that this equation has created significant success for me and clients around the world that I have helped as a coach.

I know that creating a result is not just about a visible or tangible outcome. Every success or failure affects our lives in many ways. "Results" are both external and internal. The most important results are those in the heart and mind.

Often, regardless of whether the external result was achieved, the powerful changes that take place in a person because of the effort and process, far outweigh any benefit realized or cost required by the external process.

The ultimate result that we create is the life that we live in. While "The Results Equation™ has been and will continue to apply to personal goals, corporate achievement, sports success, leadership triumph and every other visible activity, its most important application is providing the principles and power to shape your life according to your desires.

Because external manifestations are easiest to explain, see and quantify, they constitute many of the examples in the book. The true measure of the power of an individual and of the results equation is how you use it to create your life.

Part I of the book is about change. What causes it, from both external and internal perspectives? External triggers, however dramatic they may be, are only the starting point for further results that become needed or desired. Internal triggers come at any time, sometimes related to outside events and sometimes from the heart. The causes of both internal and external triggers matter.

Part II describes the results equation in detail and gives you the principles and steps required to understand this equation and see the possibilities.

Part III highlights examples of situations where the results equation has been applied or could be applied to create the change or outcome you want.

I hope this book helps you approach results you want with new vigor and determination. Read it and do the exercises with an open mind and a desire to discover and simplify the process of both creating change and managing the bumps along the road to growth.

Prologue

I stood in the meeting room staring into the faces of the engineers on my staff and the attorneys who were assembled to talk about our new project. I was the Assistant Deputy Minister of the Electricity Division at the Alberta Department of Energy. For those not familiar with government structure, that meant I was entirely in charge and solely responsible for this work.

We had been given the assignment to create a massive piece of legislation that would divide the regulating structure for all utilities in the province of Alberta, Canada. The existing commission, the Alberta Energy and Utilities Board (AEUB) had been in service for years and had done a great job, mostly.

Alberta is a province rich in oil and gas, and consequently, the AEUB had focused mainly on oil and gas drilling, permitting, compensation and safety. It also enforced the structure expressed in the law to collect mineral royalties that were a large part of provincial revenue.

Almost as a sideline, the AEUB also regulated electricity, natural gas, water, phone, and other public services.

A few years earlier, the province had decided to deregulate the electricity market similar to what had been done with the natural gas market some years earlier. Electricity is far more challenging to regulate than natural gas.

Without getting into all the technical details, the easiest way to understand the difference is that electricity can't be stored and is produced the instant you use it. That fact alone makes it extremely difficult to allow market forces to manage the provision of service. The disasters in California with Enron and other market participants bore ample testimony to the problems.

Combining the nature of electricity with the fact that there is an "unwritten social policy" that everyone has a "right" to electricity at a reasonable cost, makes the problem that much thornier.

As the deregulation processes had unfolded over the course of several years, the AEUB had been completely overwhelmed in trying to manage a deregulated electricity market with its small utilities division.

The AEUB had neither the expertise or the experience to do the job. Over the previous three years, many controversial and ill-advised decisions had distorted prices and gouged customers in the Alberta electricity market.

The politics were poison, and the market players that were profiting were claiming a "right" to a perpetuation of the current broken system with all its loopholes and advantages.

To remedy the problems a decision was made to create the "Alberta Utilities Commission" to handle all of the "utilities" in the province. The intent was to bring the expertise and focus necessary to manage the regulated and deregulated portions of all the commodities.

The need was well understood, and the engineers and attorneys knew what the job was. They were focused and excited at the opportunity to be part of such ground-breaking work. It isn't often that one participates in creating that kind of change.

A complete restructuring of public-service elements of this magnitude was a high-profile, contentious and lengthy process. It required public consultation, stakeholder groups, and significant outreach because of the far-reaching consequences and political implications.

Because of the inherent controversy, many politicians were anxious at the prospect of such a change. Obviously, they were worried about their re-election. Given such a scope, a process like this would typically take 2 to 3 years to complete.

What I had not yet told the assembled crew was that we had 60 days to get this done. The minister had told me he wanted to take it to the current legislative session because of the level of crisis already causing significant problems.

The meeting went fine until I dropped the bomb. I told them we had 60 days. Silence reigned, the color drained from all the faces, and then all hell broke loose. A whirlwind of complaints, exclamations of "impossible," and general refusal to acknowledge even the slightest possibility of achieving such a deadline, ensued.

I had expected this reaction, and so I waited until the noise in the room died down. This was just one more example of the kinds of impossible projects I had come to relish in my career.

Part I

Why Do Things Change?

Change is the natural order of things. Everything in nature sprouts, grows, matures and then dies. On a larger scale, planets, stars, and even galaxies follow the same pattern. People do the same thing. Animals all have a "cycle of life."

On top of that, we humans want to make things change in ways to our liking. We want to create structures according to our will to simplify and beautify our lives. We want to build things to make life more fun.

We are driven to explore the frontiers of the planet, the ocean, outer space, inner space, technology and every other boundary we can find. We want to grow and develop personally and express the gifts and talents we have. We want to build the new and repair the old, whether that be buildings, technology or personal relationships and habits.

Animals have instincts that cause them to do similar things. Beavers build dams and birds build nests. All these behaviors are part of the cycle of life and create change.

Change can be imposed upon us or can come from within us.

In this part, we will survey the natural and human-made forces that impose change in our lives and the world. We will mention changes that spring from internal forces and desires. We will also talk about forces that impede change, provide inertia and make things stay the same.

In the end, we know the world and the universe will never stay the same. Stuff changes no matter how hard we try to prevent it. So, the choice is simple.

We can try to understand change, work to focus and direct it for our benefit, or we can fight tooth and nail to keep things precisely as they are.

Sometimes it's better to change and sometimes it's better to work on keeping things in the current equilibrium. I would argue that even in the second case, the force of change is still at work.

The amount of effort, awareness, and energy required to keep the status quo represents a substantial change in and of itself.

Whether natural forces impose change, human-made forces or it's something we choose in our hearts, the process of changing our present circumstance to a desired future follows a very predictable pattern. This is good and lets us tackle any challenge that comes our way.

In any case, understanding this similarity and removing the mystery will lay the foundation for Part II, where we explore the creation of "The Results Equation™," and Part III where we examine ways to apply it intentionally for our benefit.

Chapter 1

Why "Do" Anything at All?

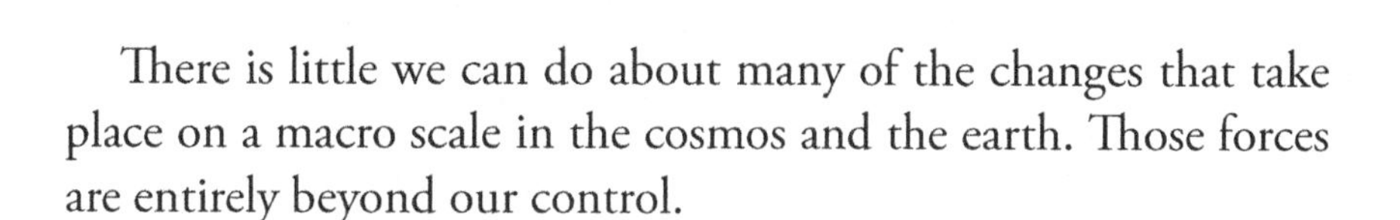

There is little we can do about many of the changes that take place on a macro scale in the cosmos and the earth. Those forces are entirely beyond our control.

Many of these laws and forces are barely understood. All we do is dabble at the fringes. One could easily ask, "Why do anything at all?"

This is mostly a philosophical question, and my purpose is not to debate answers at that scope. So, while we can't control many forces around us, we do control what we do when external things happen.

It's also true that we influence many things that affect our lives. Sometimes this influence works for good and sometimes not so much.

For example, we tinker with plant genetics. The purpose is to make plants more productive and to grow more in less space. Our tinkering sometimes screws things up; like nutritional value and the ability of plants to adapt to disease or other threats.

A spectacular example is a banana. We have, over time, selectively bred bananas for looks and longevity. In the process, we may be close to wiping out the species altogether – a world without the banana.

We do the same thing with animals used for food. Antibiotics and hormones given to farm animals cause faster growth, more milk production, and other seemingly positive benefits, but have effects on humans that we are barely beginning to understand.

We explore ways to prolong human life. We tamper with cloning and with gene splicing and other pieces of genetic engineering that some people consider unethical while others hail these efforts as game-changing.

It's in our nature to be curious and to see what we can accomplish. Many things have the desired outcome, and many create disasters. There is nothing that will stop the curiosity and experimental nature of the human spirit.

So, the idea of doing nothing is off the table. A better question might be "What things are important to explore and change?" Answers will differ depending on perspective, but whatever you decide to do, having an efficient way to create a result will be beneficial.

We can't change everything, and our ability to control some things is limited. This brings us to the inevitable conclusion that the energy and effort we do spend must be intentional and focused.

Our unending curiosity and powerful capabilities bear the greatest fruit when we purposely consider and carefully decide where to direct our efforts to create change.

Why do anything at all? Because we can. Intentional and focused effort can create longer life, greater comfort, discoveries, more fun, beautiful art, glorious music and a thousand other things manifested by the gifts and talents of every person.

In my long career as a change agent, both to create outcomes and manage processes, I have discovered that some fundamental principles and methods make exploring, creating and adapting to change more effective and powerful.

Doing nothing is always an option, but rarely is it an effective option. Standing around and letting things happen to us doesn't usually create the desired result.

Another answer to "Why do anything at all?" is that we learn through doing. We develop and discover new possibilities and opportunities that were invisible before we started.

As noted above, it's also true that changing things involves risk. It may bring unintended consequences. A willingness to act and adapt allows our unending curiosity and drive to be focused and productive as well as fun.

Over the next few chapters, we'll talk about a few reasons things change, sometimes of their own accord or due to natural processes and sometimes because we do it on purpose. This will lay the framework for the creation of the Results Equation, in Part II.

Chapter 2

Change from Natural Process

Starting at one macro level, the most obvious driver for change is nature itself. Every single element of the earth is in a state of constant change. Things are always growing or decaying.

While this might be obvious to you, I'm going to list some examples, so that it's clear how pervasive change is in the universe around us.

Every living thing has a beginning. Seeds sprout or an egg is fertilized. A single cell begins the process of division. Something triggers this cycle, and a "birth" takes place.

Every plant develops and reaches toward the sun. Every animal goes through embryonic development and ultimately encounters the world after leaving its mother.

Plants mature, and based on triggers we study but don't fully understand; they produce fruit that contains the seeds of their perpetuation. Eventually, with seasonal changes and sometimes across many years, plants get old and die.

Besides that, periodic externalities like fires, parasites, and other disasters shape forests and vegetation destructively. However, each destruction carries the seeds of new life and growth.

In the animal kingdom, we see the same thing. A litter of pups or cubs is born. After "growing up," they move to a stage of reproduction and perpetuate the species. All these things require changes and new processes in the body.

Humans also follow this process, with a major exception. Because of self-awareness and the spark born of our divine heritage, we spend a great deal of effort in trying to understand and manage the changes around us. For example, we obsess to a degree with extending life and counteracting the effects of aging and death.

If we get a little bigger and move from the things on the earth to the earth itself, we see similar processes. In much longer geologic cycles, tectonic action creates the birth of a mountain range, the birth of a river, of a lake and other formations.

Other geologic forces such as wind, rain, climate variations, earthquakes, volcanoes and the sheer power of time itself reshape the earth in massive ways. Rivers dig canyons and earthquakes create mountains, which eventually erode into plateaus and prairies.

On an even grander scale, in the universe, stars are continually being born in a fiery and amazing process involving gravity, hydrogen and other forces not well understood. The fuel burns, and ultimately in timeframes measuring billions of years, stars collapse and die.

The same holds for galaxies and other even larger mega-structures we are just beginning to identify with the powerful telescopes created to examine and understand this astounding process of change.

This natural cycle is universal and unending.

What does all this have to do with you and I creating results we want? Simply this. Whether we move into action as a result of forces we don't control or start from a desire to make something new, the process of making things happen is the same.

One learning from understanding the natural process of change is flexibility. The variety and adaptability of natural changes are incredible. That would indicate that a stance of flexibility is more productive than one of rigidity.

Adaptability, flexibility and being open to possibilities are all approaches to achievement we learn from natural processes. Noticing this will benefit our efforts to create the results we desire.

Chapter 3

External Change Forces

Moving away from natural forces outside of our control, we see change driven by structures and institutions that are our own creation.

For example, the economy might change and dramatically affect our ability to make a living. The need for specific skills may completely vanish. That happened recently with advances in technology and will likely occur again even faster as knowledge advances.

Today, climate change is a heated point of debate. Local, national and global efforts to alter the way we interact with the earth and its resources have started, been abandoned and then begun again.

Atmospheric changes such as the hole in the ozone layer drove laws and regulations that created changes in products and services that affected our lives. That change had the intended results, and recent studies indicated that the hole in the ozone layer is shrinking.

Some events like earthquakes and volcanoes not only wreak havoc and destruction in a physical sense but also create major economic consequences, social upheaval, political instability, and other changes.

Social attitudes can change quickly or over time. We no longer tolerate once accepted behaviors. This requires every individual to change or expect and cope with the consequences of remaining the same.

Political and societal changes such as views on social policy can drive large-scale change. Often prevailing views depend on elections and political cycles and therefore vary constantly.

Changes that vacillate create instability and a real sense of powerlessness. We feel like we are floundering in the wind and have no real bearings. When too many things happen at the same time, again there is a feeling of powerlessness and loss of control.

Even as turbulent times drive significant change in society, they can also cause individual instability and uncertainty. This feels confusing and like nothing is permanent or matters.

There are many more examples of changes caused by our choices as a species that drive consequences large and small. Examples include deforestation, rising ocean levels, over-farming, genetic experimentation of all kinds, poverty levels and a hundred other changes driven by technology, greed, government policy and all the rest.

Regardless of the source of the change, individually, we have the same choice. Tolerate what is or make a plan to create a desired future state. The beauty of human potential is that no matter what happens, we can build and carry out a plan to improve where we are.

Chapter 4

Internal Change Forces

As if that were not enough, internal landscapes can change just as dramatically. Life experiences can demolish long-held beliefs in an instant. Consider a few examples:

Relationship failures often mark a significant turning point in a person's view of opportunity, stability, and prospects. Those changes might be felt immediately or result in deep and lifelong scars.

Betrayal in business might cause financial ruin and drive the need to start over. It might also make a person rethink their whole approach to life – just when you thought it was all tuned up.

Dramatic spiritual experiences such as the near-death experience I had in June 2018, permanently change how we understand ourselves, God and the infinite. After such an experience, nothing is the same and your whole approach to life changes.

Sudden illness, either physical or mental, presents an unexpected challenge. These situations force us to rethink plans we had for the present and the future.

Sudden economic changes, like winning the lottery or a complete loss of life savings, are more examples of radical and intense events that force us to change.

Sometimes gradual growth and life experience completely change the nature of the relationship between marriage partners, business partners, family members or friends.

Personal growth changes may have been intentional, but the consequences are unpredictable because we never know how others will view what we have become.

There are hundreds of other forces, obvious and hidden, that operate in the complex realm of the mind and heart. Sometimes we see them coming, and sometimes we don't. All of them can drive change.

Even though internal changes might feel different than change imposed from the outside, we still have the same choice. Tolerate what is or make a plan to create a desired future state.

Your opportunity to define and create your future remains intact no matter how the present circumstance came about. The beauty of your possibility is that no matter where you are now, you can make and carry out a plan to create a new future.

Chapter 5

Pain

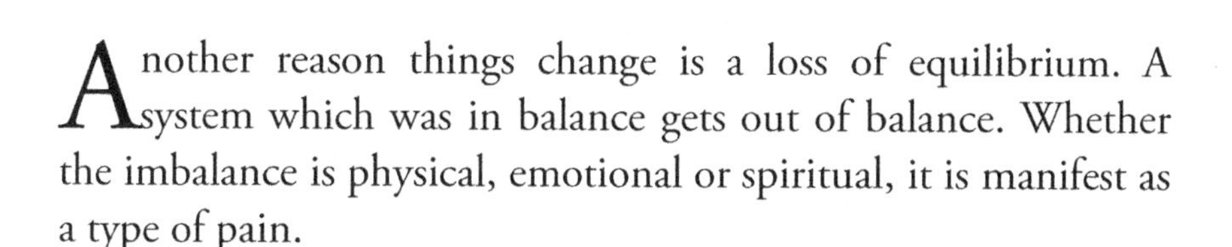

Another reason things change is a loss of equilibrium. A system which was in balance gets out of balance. Whether the imbalance is physical, emotional or spiritual, it is manifest as a type of pain.

Our foot hurts so we explore orthotics then eventually visit the doctor to figure out what's wrong and how we can fix the problem.

The roof leaks and we don't like the drip from the ceiling. We are worried about ruining the house, so we take immediate and hopefully successful corrective action to stop it.

We have a vague sense of emptiness and loneliness. We seek relief through companionship, diversion, entertainment or more destructive means like alcohol or drugs.

Some type of pain creates the drive to explore the options for change and think about the path out of the situation.

Since this kind of change always starts with an individual choice, here are some pain points that are often the starting point for a change process:

- I'm broke and need more money.
- I'm overweight and need to get in shape.
- I'm tired of working for someone else.
- I hate my boss and need a new job.
- I'm miserable and want to be happy.
- I can't stand my spouse, friend, etc. and need to end this relationship.
- I don't want more arguments and need to fix this relationship.
- My job is going away; I want a new career.
- My car is too old; I want a new car.
- I've been stuck here for years; I want a promotion.
- It's too late. My life is ruined. What now?
- My kids won't listen. They need help.
- I don't like the IRS. I can't pay my taxes.
- The government takes all my money. What's the use?
- I want to prepare for retirement.
- I can never forgive them.
- I'm never at peace.
- I don't understand why God allows this.
- The list goes on forever and ever.

Whatever the pain point, when it gets severe enough, we do one of two things. We give up and resign ourselves to complain and suffer with what is, or, we take action and try to make something happen.

When resignation is the answer, sometimes we lash out emotionally or physically and do something stupid. Or, we adopt bad habits to numb the feeling of failure.

When we take action, we immediately have a small sense of power, and if things move in a good direction at all, we keep at it for a while.

How long we keep moving depends on how bad the pain is and how much effort is needed to create the change we seek.

Without effective goals and measurements and continued motivation, the effort at change usually stops as soon as the worst of the pain is managed.

Though far from ideal, we settle into a new equilibrium and limp along until the problem is once again too intense – then the cycle repeats.

Chapter 6

Desire

One of the greatest forces for change is desire. We want something different than what we have right now. Many of the problems in the chapter on "pain," may also create a direct desire for a new situation.

A desire to create change can come from anything. You can watch a movie or read a book and then have a sudden realization that changing some aspect of your life seems beneficial.

You can go to a concert or conference and experience a new opportunity or a different way of thinking that causes you to reflect and then creates a desire.

When I ask someone "What do you want?" Desires I often hear include:

- More money.
- More happiness.
- More peace.

- More time.
- Less stress.
- A different living situation.
- A new house.
- A new relationship with God.
- A new life partner.
- A new sense of accomplishment.
- A new feeling of peace.
- Overcome an addiction.
- Start a business.
- Expressing a particular talent.
- Help others.
- Time to pursue a hobby.
- Time to spend with family.
- Experience a huge achievement.
- And a hundred variations.

Most of the time, the desires remain merely wishes. They come expressed with wistfulness and resignation that feels like "I know I can't really have this, at least not like I want, but I want it badly."

The reason they remain only wishes is that there is no follow-up. There is NO clarity to the vision, no plan, no accountability, no rewards, and no deadlines. One critical element to measure the power of the desire comes from another question. This second question is "Why do you want that?"

The first answer I hear no matter the expressed desire is usually – "Because it will make my life better."

Follow-up questions like "Exactly what will be different?" Or, "Why will this make your life better?" usually haven't been thoroughly thought out. Often the feeling is pretty simple. "Well, obviously if I had more money, life would be easier."

Of course, it's not obvious. Some people are very poor and happy, and some are very rich and miserable. There are those who inherit great wealth or win the lottery and in a short time find themselves destitute.

Having no concrete or specific reason for an objective is a key indicator that the desire is shallow.

Once in a while, I will meet someone who has a well thought out goal. They know exactly what they want and why they want it. They can describe precisely what this achievement will bring and the difference it will make for themselves.

That is a great starting point because that kind of desire is far more powerful than a vague wish. Creating and then harnessing that powerful desire will be explored later in the book.

Chapter 7

Money, Status and Power

Sometimes the desire for change is driven by the perceived "need" for wealth, status or power. Stories of the rich and famous create a false sense of ease and fun that seems to come if you have a lot of cash.

In some ways, the words "status" and "wealth" are used interchangeably, but I'm going to differentiate them in this chapter.

Wealth is the accumulation of money. Someone that has "more money" often seems to be accorded privileges and access that those without money don't have. This is not always true, but it may feel like that's the case if you have never had "more money."

Money is a driver for people who believe that it provides life with less stress, less turmoil, more access, fewer hours working and possession of the "luxuries" of life. Money can buy things. Money can buy vacations. Money can buy property.

We all know money can't buy love and we know that money alone while facilitating certain aspects of life, can be a big hindrance. Money by itself does not provide a sustainable engine for real change.

The desire for "more money" can last for a while and cause extraordinary things to happen, but in the end, pure money motivation is hollow and fails.

Status is another of those imaginary things. Sports stars, movie stars and others who are in the public eye are accorded a certain status and privilege.

Often status comes with money, but they are not the same. Status can also come from being a television personality. Ask any news anchor. They are indeed well known and have a perceived status but not much money.

A burning desire for status can drive behaviors and even aggressive change. However, status is often one of those things that once achieved, feels hollow. Typically it doesn't present the satisfaction you thought it would while you were chasing it.

Power is different from both money and status. Power is the ability to get things done. Often "power" is defined as the authority to require other people to do things, like in a company hierarchy. Power has many other definitions and forms. Sometimes power comes with money or status, but not always.

A desire for power can drive change in an individual, or a group. It can start a movement or a revolution. The effects and duration of power often depend on its use. In the end, power is like status or money. After you get it, it seems like it has somehow changed shape. It doesn't look as good from the inside.

I have taken this journey. I was seduced by the desire for all three at different points in my life. Coming from a place of "perceived lack," where I lacked money, had no status and little power, at least in my mind, I went to a position of significant wealth, highly acknowledged status and considerable power. At least it was so in my little pond.

Predictably, I overestimated the value and grossly exaggerated how good the acquisition of these things would feel. I became overwhelmed by the emptiness of the accomplishment. Then, I abandoned it all and trashed my life.

I was a miserable poster child for having my drivers for change be wealth, status and power.

To be clear, I am not saying that wealth, status or power are somehow evil. I am saying that as drivers for change, they are insufficient for the long run. We must anchor ourselves in something deeper for the changes to be beneficial and permanent.

Chapter 8

So, What?

The preceding chapters have been a brief survey of causes of change. Some changes are imposed externally and unexpectedly by natural or human-made events. Some changes come from inside. Any of them may manifest gradually or suddenly.

Some are carefully planned. Some come because we want something, we fear something, or we want our circumstance to be different.

There are two points here. First, regardless of the cause, we regularly want to respond to our circumstance. We want to make something different than it is at this moment.

Second, we must understand our relationship to change. When we want something to be different than it is now, what are the attitudes, stories, skills, and powers that we bring to the situation?

Here are the facts:

- Natural change around us takes place no matter what we do.
- Scientific advancement and change occur outside our wishes or control.

- Environmental change comes independently of our wishes and behavior.
- Relationship changes happen, sometimes by choice, sometimes by the choices of others.
- We have no power over the behavior of others.
- We have no power over cosmic forces.
- We have little to no power over societal dynamics.
- We may achieve power and influence in some situations for a short period, but in the big scheme of things what we do usually doesn't change the world very much.
- The list is long and seemingly overwhelming.

If that's true, then we're back to the question from the beginning. "Why do anything at all?" The answer is still the same. Because you can. What you do control is who you are and how you show up in the world.

This is the founding principle. You control every single experience in your life. This is true notwithstanding the externalities that happen "to you." You have exactly the life you want no matter what happens around you.

I started the section with large-scale circumstances and changes. I meant to be inclusive and sweeping. It's those events where we often feel the most powerless.

The way we control our lives most fundamentally is to intentionally choose how we *experience* life around us and how we *act*, independent of external events and realities.

A simple example will illustrate. Two people get pushed into a swimming pool. One laughs, realizing there's nothing they can do and goes with the situation. The other rages and chafes because they will be late for an interview.

The external event is the same; the internal experience they have inside is the opposite. The creator of the experience is the person who chooses.

For the forces you do control and the things you want to create, how you approach them in attitude and focus determines your experience and therefore your life.

Because that is true, the experience along the way is yours to create whether you achieve a specific goal or not.

Another example will illustrate.

Two people have shovels and dig an irrigation ditch across a yard. One is resentful and angry, rages about what else they could be doing and has a generally crappy experience but completes the project anyway. The other creates a masterpiece, is proud of his workmanship and enjoys the day.

Both created the outcome. The experience of each person was completely different.

This is the critical point. The attitude or "context," you bring to a situation determines not only the experience but is often decisive as to whether you even complete the goal.

Those who come from a negative place are more easily distracted, more easily delayed and often do a poor job. When you find every aspect of the project onerous, the barriers can seem so large that the effort fails.

Those who choose to bring positive energy and attitude to the situation are more creative, faster in completing the work and finish projects with more energy and power.

Whatever the event, something builds a desire to create a new reality. Whether we are responding to externalities or creating internal goals, we want something different.

Let's define "achievement," to mean "an outcome we want to create through the intentional process of making a change."

This achievement might be a remedy for something that happened around us, or it might be responding to an inner longing and vision. Either way, it's now a considered choice based on a decision-making process.

Now that you want to create something, what happens next is all a function of your current situation, your desired future and the choices you make to create movement.

After we decide we want something and think about what that achievement will look like, we come face to face with another reality. Setting aside things you don't control; we have barriers and obstacles that stand in the way of doing things you *do* control.

In other words, we all set goals and fail. We start to do something with the best of intentions and then fall short and give up.

Why do we "settle" for far less than we could otherwise achieve?

Chapter 9

Achievement Barriers

Watch little children at play. One child playing with blocks will repeatedly try to create a stack as high as they can. Perhaps the goal is to use all the blocks; maybe the goal is to build up far enough to knock it down.

Regardless of the goal, and without heeding the number of times that poor block placement causes the tower to fall, the child enjoys the process and sits playing with the blocks for a long time.

Another child, with a different approach, exhibits frustration when the blocks don't stack. Perhaps the placement is uneven, so the structure falls quickly. Tears flow, frustration mounts, the child knocks the blocks across the room, and the situation is anything but fun.

The setup is the same, but the experience of the child is quite different. Your heart is moved as you feel the frustration of the child. You might wonder at the same time, why he or she can't just have fun playing with the blocks?

When we go about creating an achievement, we also have real and perceived barriers to success and enjoyment of the process. Here are some examples of events and situations that make achievement hard or easy:

- Looming deadlines create stress.
- Financial pressures create stress.
- Personal expectations create stress.
- Misunderstanding boundaries and objectives create stress.
- Bad instructions create apathy and frustration.
- Small setbacks create project abandonment.
- Having no deadlines at all creates laziness.
- Having a bad day creates stress.
- Previous failures create negativity.
- Previous successes create confidence.
- Having a great day creates excitement.
- Small successes increase enthusiasm.
- Having a sizeable impending reward creates excitement.
- Anticipating massive recognition creates enthusiasm.

A hundred other things, both positive and negative, affect how we think about, engage with and ultimately do or don't achieve the objective in front of us.

What are the barriers that prevent us from choosing objectives, starting down the path of achievement and finishing by creating the outcome we intended?

Further to that and regardless of the deadlines, stress creators or enticements, what prevents us from engaging in the process in the most effective way while getting to the end?

Each person is different, and we could blame "temperament, personality and habit" for one person's perseverance versus another person's willingness to give up at the first setback. But, that would be way too easy. There are many things at work here, and each plays a significant role in causing success or failure.

As a long-time consultant called in to do "impossible" tasks and a business and performance coach for the last ten years, I have noticed common barriers that prevent even the best-intended projects from getting completed.

I have also noticed common characteristics and habits that create encouragement, perseverance, and support efforts to finish, despite overwhelming opposition. There are a hundred variations of each of the barriers I'll list, so don't be disappointed if this list doesn't contain your favorite flavor.

Your choice is to find yourself in the list and create a strategy to identify and change the areas of challenge or to make excuses why "you are different," and why nothing can explain or alleviate your particular situation.

You know where that second choice inevitably leads. Stagnation, inaction and ultimately to an abandonment of goals and dreams. With a commitment to discovery and change in mind, let's take a look in the next few chapters at some common barriers.

Chapter 10

Fear

Fear is one of the most pervasive, pernicious and powerful barriers that get in the way of getting to the achievements we set out to reach.

It has many names and comes from many places. Your flavor will be unique to you. Here are some familiar sources of fear that I hear repeated over and over again in my coaching practice.

- Fear of failure.
- Fear of rejection.
- Fear of looking stupid.
- Fear of being laughed at.
- Fear of "what, you didn't know how to do that?"
- Fear of the unknown.
- Fear of dying. (Often masked as a fear of loss or a fear of change.)
- Fear of losing a relationship.

- Fear of losing money.
- Fear of staying broke.
- Fear of success.
- Fear of changing.
- Fear of losing favor.
- Fear of being exposed as a fraud.
- Fear of weakness.
- Fear of admission of weakness.
- Fear of needing help.
- Fear of the truth.
- Fear of lies.
- Fear of standing out.
- Fear of never making it.
- Fear of a hundred other things.

If you think about it for a moment, you will be amazed at the number of ways fear has interfered with your ability to be your best self. It can be frustrating to take stock of how fear has prevented you from discovering, developing and manifesting your divine nature and gifts.

Regardless of how fear has impacted you in the past, spending a lot of time with regrets and being frustrated won't change anything. What's essential is knowing there is a way past this. There's a way to acknowledge fears you have, manage them, eliminate them, work through them and achieve your objectives.

Where does all this fear come from? This is not a psychology book, but what I see is that they come from many places. Examples might include:

- Childhood memories.
- Styles of parenting you had.
- The kind of bosses you had.
- Successes you had.
- Failures you had.
- Times you were betrayed.
- Times you betrayed others.
- Times you created wealth.
- Times you experienced poverty.
- Situations where you were embarrassed.
- Situations where you imagined you might be embarrassed.
- Situations where others were embarrassed or ridiculed.
- Times you were punished.
- Times you were bullied or threatened.
- A hundred other past experiences.

An interesting commonality of the sources of fear is that they are all based in the past. Even things that you equate with fear have roots in the memories that real or perceived events left behind.

Whether you experienced something yourself or saw another's experience, it's still in the past.

Whether you imagined fear or heard of others' fear, your reaction is an anticipated consequence with its roots in your past or your story about someone else's past.

Even fear of the unknown comes principally because previous experience with the unknown or uncertain has somehow been negative.

You know this because as you watch a child, they joyfully and fearlessly experiment and try new things until their experience teaches them to fear the future.

For example, when I was learning to ski at age 45, my innate fear of getting hurt made me slow and hesitant as I forced myself to do more difficult runs every time I went to the ski hill. I struggled to get past the black and then into double black runs.

On the other hand, my teenage children threw themselves into the very same hills and dealt with the inevitable tumbles and crashes in a different psychological way.

My fear of potentially hurting myself inhibited my learning and performance. Their certainty that they wouldn't permanently hurt anything created a different path. Regardless of falls, they believed it was more fun to "get after it."

I was in good health, in good shape and quite capable. Nevertheless, the head game gave them a completely different experience: same hill, same ski instructor, same day, a different outlook.

One important exercise is to thoughtfully and truthfully explore five current activities or projects where fear is impeding your progress. Perhaps you aren't moving fast enough. Maybe you keep procrastinating.

Take time to do this exercise when there's no pressure and no rush. Experiment with telling the truth. Fear may prevent you from telling the truth because you may be afraid of admitting weakness. Experience that feeling and make the list. You can burn it later if you need to.

Chapter 11

Technology

Technology is the collection of knowledge and tools that allow us to navigate everyday life. From computers to human-made materials to agricultural innovations to advances in understanding the body and the brain – technology is the way these things are expressed and used in the world.

Technology is also a barrier to achievement. When new things come into existence or old things are used in a profoundly new way, we have a choice. Continue doing what we've done or adopt new knowledge and tools.

A classic example is the story of John Henry, who according to legend, died with his hammer in his hand in a contest with the new technology of the time, the steam drill. I won't repeat the story here, but it is worth a google search. The story is fantastic and the legend compelling, but the point is that the introduction of technology created a problem.

Today, technology changes rapidly and profoundly. A few years ago, it used to be common and a little funny if someone said:

"I'm just not tech savvy and don't know how to use a computer." People would smile or smirk at that and think it quaint or cute.

Today that's not funny. It's a barrier to fully engaging in many aspects of life, and the person who's not willing to learn to use new technology is often ignored and marginalized.

The actual barrier to achievement is not the technology itself. Technology is often an expression of other changes and developments. It becomes a barrier to creating results when there is a lack of skill using it or a lack of willingness to learn.

If we expand the idea of technology into "any method, system or tool designed to get something done," then technology is not just gadgets and physical objects but processes and systems as well.

Resisting technology can be a big barrier to achievement. The biggest problem, of course, is not the technology and the new landscape it creates, but our attitude about whether we're willing to develop the knowledge and skill to use it.

Another way technology impedes achievement is through infatuation. If we become infatuated with the latest gadgets and gear, then we can get lost in the trees and miss the forest of opportunity that may be sitting in front of us.

I've had clients who are so caught up in staying current with the latest applications, software, and innovations that they regularly get sidetracked and don't accomplish the goals they have proclaimed are essential. Managing this distraction is another needed skill.

Technology, either as a system or a gadget, is fundamentally a tool. It's designed to facilitate a process – either to do it better or to do something new that couldn't be done before.

If we remember its status as a tool and use it productively and positively, and as long as we remember it is a means to an end and not the end in itself, then technology doesn't need to be a barrier to achievement.

In making choices about adopting technology, there's a simple question. "Will the time, energy and money required to learn and deploy the technology be repaid in efficiency, output or reduced effort?" This is a classic question about return on investment or return on invested time.

The key to all this is the attitude we bring to the situation. If we bring fear, self-doubt, and accumulation of excuses, then technology is a barrier. Fear of failing, fear of being too slow, fear of being embarrassed and other fears listed in the last chapter also delay or prevent learning.

If we bring curiosity, determination, and excitement, then we can make choices about technology that are beneficial and help us achieve the results we desire.

Chapter 12

External Norms

This is a broad topic with many individual pieces. Religion, nationality, gender, race, family tradition, community tradition and variations of all these carry their own sets of expectations and rules that can be barriers to achievement.

Every religion has its dogma and a set of dos and don'ts. Some religions teach that man is inherently bad and always will be. Seeking "achievement" might, therefore, be perceived as suspect with an uncertain and potential unsuccessful outcome.

Other belief systems place man as supreme with no accountability to a higher power. That would produce an entirely different set of challenges as such a person might create opposition and trouble by trampling over others on the way to success.

Historically, in many cultures, women were treated as the "weaker sex." In other cultures, women were revered as wiser and therefore given leadership responsibilities. Each of these views creates challenges for both sexes in creating results.

Even today, there is a great deal of cultural upheaval about equality, opportunity and the achievement of goals related to the issues surrounding gender.

Early explorers discovered native populations in "new" lands. Existing governments and religious bodies "back home" debated about whether these new individuals were even human. This might seem unthinkable now, but today, bias, prejudice and socialization still create huge barriers to the achievement cycle.

History is replete with thousands of examples of traditions and norms that make "achievement," or doing something new and different, more complicated than necessary. At worst, such systems represent a huge impediment to even considering different results than the status quo.

The existence of all these mythologies, traditions, norms and assumptions is pervasive. It's not conceivable to invent a world without them. The key is that *it is not necessary to eliminate them to master the art of achievement.*

These norms and attitudes themselves are not barriers. The barriers arise from not considering that the "old way" is no longer functional. What once seemed right may no longer be relevant. Again, we come face to face with the truth that our attitude is the determining factor in creating our achievement and therefore our lives.

For example, we used to treat certain diseases by letting blood. Over time, it became clear that this method wasn't effective. With great trepidation and much resistance, that medical norm was abandoned in favor of new techniques.

What do we do to stay out of these traps? We must understand the relationship of our existing beliefs or "context" to achieving new and different results. This understanding has three parts.

First, these norms and traditions exist and can't be ignored. They often seem woven into the fabric of our DNA. It's easy to be oblivious to them and treat them as an unchangeable reality even though they are traditions. Step one is acknowledging their existence and the need for examination.

Even though we view such traditions as inviolable, they are, in fact, the accumulation of how we've experienced life. Undoubtedly, they functioned very well in certain circumstances and at certain times.

The truth is that most of the time, the beliefs we have are not universally true. They may need to be examined and appropriately modified to create the achievement we seek. This is easy to say and profoundly difficult to accomplish, especially when talking about one's internal belief system.

For example, if you have the story that animals aren't clean and carry disease, then you won't want to have a house pet. If you grew up with a cat sleeping on your bed every night, you laugh at such an idea and view someone who holds that belief with suspicion and worry.

If your goal requires a change to your long-standing belief about animals, and you want to become someone who has pets, you must address the source, reasonableness, and consequences of making that change.

For example, I never lived with an animal indoors. My mom thought they were dirty and belonged outside, even though she grew up on a farm. My wife always had indoor cats who were part of the intimate family.

Getting used to joyfully accepting piles of cat hair and scratched up furniture was a change I made as a trade for the beauty, love, and companionship I get from the relationship. This may seem like a trivial example, but the principles involved are exactly the same for addressing any belief that impedes your desired achievement.

Second, what you have now is the result of what you do now. Another simple statement with profound implications. Said another way, the system of beliefs and behaviors you exhibit today created your existence today. If you want a different result, you must create a different system.

If you want a small change, then the shift in the system might be minor. Often, we're looking for substantial changes like big shifts in income, major upgrades in happiness or marked improvements in health or relationships.

If the size of your goal is significant, you may have big changes to make. An excellent place to start looking for opportunity is the beliefs and behaviors that got you where you are.

What is your existing relationship to the achievement or goal? Then look at other areas of your life and ask, "What is your relationship to setting goals and creating success?"

For example, if you were taught that big money belongs to "other people" and those who have it are usually bad, then you will have trouble creating cash and enjoying it.

Learning to accept and understand that every result comes from employing the system that creates that result, puts you in a more objective position to evaluate existing norms and beliefs and choosing needed changes.

Third, we tend to label norms and traditions as "good" or "bad." Changing what we have done in the past becomes more difficult if we view "different" as "wrong." Often the judgment is more effective when we view it through a lens of "functionality" instead of "morality."

This is not to say that there shouldn't be a test for integrity and morality. There is, and there should be. Too often we judge what had gone before as right, only because it has been done before. That is often ineffective and impedes progress.

The secret to working with these three elements is our starting attitude. If we view change as natural, desirable and a key to progress, then we look for ways to do it quickly and effectively. If change is scary, dangerous and regarded with suspicion, then inevitably we fail.

Chapter 13

Internal Beliefs

Even more important than the external factors of family, race, religion, tradition, nationality and all the rest, is the story you carry inside about *yourself*.

We're all familiar with situations where two siblings raised in the same family create incredibly different lives. So different that it's surprising when we find out that they come from the same background.

One is a successful executive, makes a lot of money and lives ostentatiously with all the luxuries that money can buy, and position can provide.

Another from the same family is homeless, unable to keep a job and with no obvious explanation for their diminished circumstances.

One thought might be a mental illness or some other external force. Even setting that aside, there are situations with no easy explanations. What makes such a difference?

The difference lies in the truth you choose to live with. Your "context" is the set of beliefs you carry around that shape and limit your possibilities. It is the lens through which you see the world.

I talk about that thoroughly in *The Book of Context*, where you can learn to identify and change your beliefs and limitations. Information about that book and other resources is in the Appendix.

Each of us is limited by what we believe is possible. Our reality forms itself entirely from the shape of our beliefs. For example, imagine a constraining bodysuit or straitjacket uniquely fitted to you that prevents you from doing something.

It's not that the bodysuit or straitjacket is imposed on you, it's that you accept it and live within the constraints, however uncomfortable they may be. You do that because you accept it as the boundary of what you can achieve.

You don't consider the real possibility that something greater or more significant is available. Consequently, you don't try something until you at least believe it'll work out. Without a glimmer of hope of a positive outcome, you don't expend any significant effort.

A thousand examples come to mind and here are a few:

- You don't believe you're good enough to write a book, so you don't try.
- You don't believe you have anything to say, so you don't speak.
- You don't believe you're worth it, so you don't ask for a promotion.
- You don't think you have confidence, so you don't resolve the problem.

- You've failed at something before, so you don't try again, or if you do, the effort is half-hearted and without a spark.
- You believe you'll be rejected, so rather than be humiliated, you don't do it.
- You believe something will be rejected, so as you near completion you slow down, let perfectionism take over, and never finish.
- You believe you'll be without love if you rise above the circumstances of your family, so you don't try much, and if a great opportunity presents itself, you don't take advantage of it.
- You convince yourself that if others knew "the real you," they wouldn't like you, so you stay hidden with your light turned down low.
- And on and on and on.

The truth is that you are capable of great and marvelous things. You are a divine being with infinite opportunity and significant raw talent – enough to create a masterpiece in your life.

Consider the time wasted and the energy squandered on the argument about whether to try something based on assumptions about the outcome. That energy alone could create masterpieces beyond measure. What sadness!

The barrier of internal beliefs is the *principal* cause of our lack of achievement. We can manage external barriers. Resources can be discovered and deployed. The internal landscape sets the tone, lights the fire and keeps the motor running.

Chapter 14

Pretending

A mix of external influences and internal stories creates another substantial barrier to achievement called "pretending." This act of lying, misrepresentation and false projection can take many forms. All of them pernicious and significant barriers to progress.

Here are a few:

- In my arrogance, I pretend that I'm already exactly where I want to be and don't need to try. Consequently, I remain stuck where I am while my internal compass screams for more. The resulting discord causes ulcers, misery, and life in the clutch of mediocrity.
- I can't stand the thought of anyone looking down on me, so I project to those around me, in my social media accounts and even myself, that I'm doing well. I pretend all setbacks are temporary, nothing matters, and I never tell the truth.
- I learned to lie at an early age because it kept people distant and seemed to grease the wheels of relationships. I tell people what they want to hear. Things seem to go

better, and I have fewer problems. The reality is the lies cause discord and dissonance in my heart and reduce my willingness and ability to change substantially.

- Something about change scares me so badly that I would rather live in a world of pretense. It feels safe when I don't need to do anything. I can't face the truth about what might be required to accomplish a goal that is burning in my heart.
- At the core, I've decided I am "fundamentally flawed." Because of this, I know I can never do anything awesome, so I pretend I don't want to.
- I believe that others have gifts and talents; I stand in awe and amazement at what some people are doing. I feel small and like I don't matter, so I live either in resignation, doomed to my fate, or in resentment, because I can't be "like them."
- I want to do something more with myself, and either because of fear or because it's hard, I get discouraged, and then pretend I'm too busy and put it off until later.
- I pretend I've already got what I need and don't want anything else, even though I know there is so much more I could give in service and love to those around me.

There are a hundred variations of these statements that represent the pretending in the hearts of many I know. This constraining story is not true; it is a lie. This barrier is particularly painful for me because I lived there for so long.

If you want more information about me, I wrote my story in *TightRope of Depression – My Journey from Darkness, Despair and Death to Light, Love and Life.* Details are in the Appendix.

In every case, without exception, you can be who you want, do what you want and have what you want. You create your reality and live below what is possible only because you pretend it's impossible.

What I'm saying may sound harsh when I call it a lie. Whether or not the victim statement sounds convincing or makes you sad, the real tragedy is the fact that the lie is convincing and creates a huge barrier to what you achieve.

What would happen if you made a firm and unalterable commitment to stop pretending, live in truth and focus the power and creativity you have on being the divine person that you are – instead of wasting creativity and energy dealing with the discord and pain of the story you live in?

Chapter 15

Inertia and Momentum

In physics, two principles of motion are relevant to getting an object moved from one place to another. They apply equally well in the context of achieving results.

Inertia represents the weight of a rock. It's the amount of energy it takes to cause the rock to move. It's the effort and sweat you have to put in to get it to budge.

In the context of making a change or achieving a result, inertia is the physical, emotional and spiritual energy you must put into a project before anything happens.

It's important to understand that you don't usually see outward progress immediately. The rock doesn't move *at all* until the energy put into moving it exceeds the weight or inertia of the rock.

An intangible example would be changing a relationship. The inertia or weight of the existing circumstance or "status quo" is the accumulation of past experiences, both positive and negative, that define the current state of the relationship.

That means the first attempt to change a relationship usually does nothing or appears to do nothing because it doesn't exceed the relationship inertia. Often, our first attempt at something is small, fearful and therefore ineffective.

Until the energy put into the change exceeds the inertia of the accumulated weight of past experience, there will be no difference.

Instead of thinking of this in a discouraging way, consider it a joyful reality. It easily explains why our first efforts to do something don't seem to work. It does *not* mean you will fail. It means if nothing happens the first time, then the next effort must be bigger to overcome the inertia.

Momentum is the other end of that equation. Once you've overcome the inertia of the first movement, the object now has momentum. All the energy you exerted to get the rock in motion is now stored in the rock.

Momentum is the accumulated energy that you put in to start the rock moving plus any additional energy you add after that. We sometimes say, "after we started the project, it took on a life of its own." Once a rock starts rolling, it'll continue to roll until resistance stops it.

This is precisely the same with any result you want to create. Once movement starts, you have the benefit of the accumulated energy. As long as you continue to put in the work sufficient to overcome the resistance or friction of movement, the project will keep rolling forward.

One description, which I frequently repeat through this book is this: "Once you get on a road to a destination, as long as you keep moving, you will eventually get there."

Nothing will change that reality. Once you start moving toward a goal, as long as you continue to put one foot in front of the other and do not stop moving, you will eventually reach that objective.

Understanding inertia and momentum in the physical world isn't difficult. Even if you hate physics, the equations aren't that complicated. Their function and results can be calculated and predicted.

In such equations, you can factor in the resistance provided by gravity; the force exerted on an object, the mass of the object and every other variable to understand precisely what energy causes movement and creates the desired effect.

Creating results in the intangible world is less precise and predictable. It's a little more complicated but follows the same rules. It's only our stories that cause it to be confusing.

Variables like human behavior, attitude and people changing their minds may be less predictable than the force of gravity but can still be accommodated. Sometimes we use these variables as an excuse for failure.

The truth is simpler. Even with more complex intangible variables like attitude, behavior, loyalty, emotion and externalities, achieving any result you like is possible, exhilarating and fun.

Chapter 16

OK, We're Moving, Now What?

Now we get to the fun part. If you are willing to discard old beliefs and choose to know the results you want are available, a whole new world opens to you.

If you've ever rolled a big rock down a hill, you know what an interesting set of feelings come with that experience. As a kid in Boy Scouts, we often went hiking in the mountains.

Inevitably, it would be exciting to find big rocks and roll them down a hill. There were contests to see who could get the rocks to roll the fastest and furthest.

Without debating the wisdom of rolling rocks downhill and danger of a rock smacking some unsuspecting person, rolling through a campsite or banging into a building, some parallels are useful.

Eventually, rocks rolling down a hill come to a stop. They run into a tree, the slope of the hill changes or there is enough resistance in the terrain that the rock stops.

It's rarely the case that a project you want to complete or change you want to create will keep moving of its own accord. Every goal we set, every change we try to create and every personal objective we have, faces precisely the same problem. There is resistance to change inherent in nature. The resistance comes from the inside and from outside.

Gravity provides enormous resistance that we depend on and need. Friction between the surface of the rock and the hill is a big factor. The shape of the rock is another important element. A rounded rock rolls easily and the friction is small. A rock with flat sides has huge friction and stops much sooner.

When you create a change, you will encounter the same resistance. Every habit you have and every system that is currently in place has a degree of inertia, just like a rock. Your effort to change has to overcome that inertia before any movement happens and must compensate for friction along the way.

The energy and resources you continue to put into a project or goal must be greater than the friction pushing back on the project, or it will stop moving. Many projects start well but stop when the level of ongoing work becomes apparent. I often hear, "I didn't know it was going to be *that* hard."

If you think about personal habits, this is not surprising. I call that internal resistance "spiritual gravity" or "energetic gravity." It's the analog of the physical gravity we are so familiar with.

Just like physical gravity, spiritual gravity is predictable and dependable. It operates in direct proportion to the size of the change – just like physical gravity.

If you want to start a big rock moving, it has a lot of inertia and takes a lot of pushing to get that first movement. If you have a long-standing habit that is deeply entrenched, you have the same requirement. The determination and commitment must exceed the weight of the habit.

Ask anyone who tries to quit smoking. There is a physical element, where the body craves the nicotine high, and there is a spiritual element where the body and the mind also crave the habit, the comfort and the sensation of smoking.

If you are determined to create change, your calculation as you begin must include the sustained effort required to keep the change moving until it becomes the new status quo.

There are all kinds of numbers out there about how many days you have to do something to create a new habit. I'm not going to agree with any particular number. The point here is that the effort required to change something that is a habit for you, whether it be physical or spiritual, will be substantial and require effort and consistency over time.

The answer to the question "Now what?" Is that you either continue with the required resources, including energy, time and cash or friction will stop the change you started.

There are also positive elements that contribute to sustaining the momentum created by successful change. Feedback from the consequences of the change may be encouraging. For example, you may start to feel better immediately if you begin to exercise or stop smoking.

Those incremental and intermediate experiences provide encouragement and evidence that the change you're creating is worthwhile and the goal is valuable.

As you evaluate the process of creating a result, counting the cost in time, energy and cash is a critical factor to your success. As obvious as that may be, many goals fail because this calculation is not performed or leaves out essential elements.

Now that you're moving, you either keep applying the energy and resources required to get to the goal, or you get discouraged, quit trying and flop. It sounds simple, but it's not.

Chapter 17

Here to There

Let's break this down to its purest form. No matter what your goal is, no matter what your mission is, or what you feel you must accomplish, and regardless of the area of life you focus on, achieving a goal is like making a trip.

It is the journey from "Here to There." "Here," is where you are now. How much you weigh, how much money you have, the position you hold at work, the current state of your relationship, the current state of your company's P&L, the state of your spirituality or whatever else. "Here" represents the precise condition that exists in the present.

"There," is a description of the future. The new state of your bank account, your relationship, your job at work, the new market share you have or the parameters of whatever goal you are trying to accomplish.

Clarity in these points is essential. We will explore this more fully Part II. For now, let's use a simple example: if you're trying to get to Kansas City, it's vital that you know that the destination is Kansas City and not Chicago.

Furthermore, the precise address in Kansas City is also important since the city is big and there are lots of places there that won't satisfy whatever it is that you want to do in Kansas City.

You need to know where you are today, "California," is not enough to get you moving on the right path. The route to Kansas City will be different if you start in San Diego as opposed to Sacramento. Thinking of any goal like a trip from "Here," to "There," is a simple model to create clarity and simplicity for the goal.

A quote often attributed to Albert Einstein is: "Everything should be as simple as possible, but not simpler." One attributed to Leonardo da Vinci is: "Simplicity is the ultimate sophistication." Both illustrate the need to stay away from over complication.

Another part of simplicity is to break the goal into smaller steps. You don't drive from San Diego to Kansas City without stopping. You set intermediate destinations, where you plan to stay the night.

While this seems obvious, it amazes me how often I encounter resistance to setting a smaller initial goal because somehow it feels like it's too easy, too small or doesn't matter compared to the big objective.

What matters is that you create a clear vision of where you're going, make a plan, assemble the resources, find the motivation to start the process and have provisions for inevitable roadblocks.

Every journey you want is possible. Every goal you set for yourself is achievable. However, by itself, that wisdom is inadequate. That is one reason so many goals fail, and so many people give up.

Nothing ever works exactly as planned; every goal is harder to achieve than you thought and there are always setbacks. If you have no reserve and skill to accommodate and master those inevitabilities, then your chance of success evaporates quickly.

Chapter 18

The Master Key

What is the secret? Where is the magic? What is it that separates those who achieve great things repeatedly and consistently from onlookers who blame failure on circumstance, bad luck and everything else?

Many keys unlock different parts of the achievement process. One master key is the foundation for successful application of all the tools you assemble, all the skills you learn and all the resources you accumulate.

The master key is "Taking Responsibility."

We have all heard the story of Thomas Edison and his thousands of failed attempts at creating a light bulb. We have heard many other examples of "impossible" achievements that came about solely because of commitment.

It's the same thing with your goals. No matter how many books you read, how many seminars you attend or how many motivational videos you watch, your "work" or effort is what creates success.

Your victory comes from a personal choice you make. You and you alone are responsible for the success or failure of your goals.

The bigger the goal you set out to achieve – the larger the mountains, the bigger the obstacles and the higher the uncertainty. That has always been the case and will always be true in the future.

There will always be obstacles. There will always be times when you don't think you can continue. Things sometimes work out entirely differently than you planned. There will be times when those around you tell you to stop, get in the way or actively undermine your efforts. There will be days of disappointment, frustration, and fear.

What you choose at those times is the deciding factor. The Results Equation is a powerful and successful tool that you can use in any area of your life to bring your goals into existence. However, even the best tool will only succeed when your attention, love, time and determination are the engine.

Those who look around and blame external things may get sympathy, and they may calm their conscience or smooth over their disappointment, but they will not achieve the victory. This key principle is so important; it's worth repeating.

The master key is "Taking Responsibility."

Chapter 19

The Four Questions

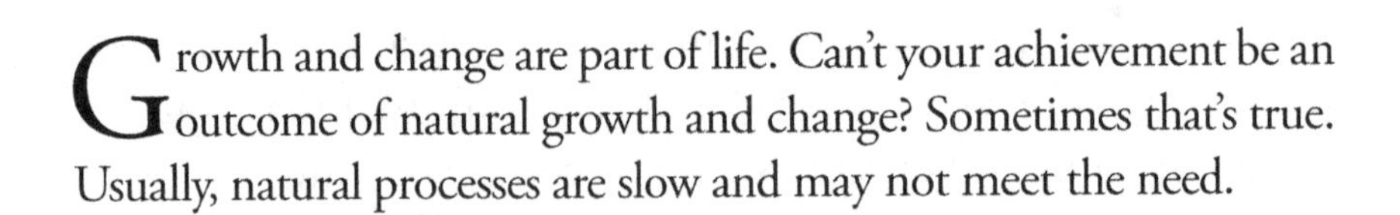

Growth and change are part of life. Can't your achievement be an outcome of natural growth and change? Sometimes that's true. Usually, natural processes are slow and may not meet the need.

At the same time, we sometimes complicate things. We act as if goals must be messy and difficult.

Every achievement breaks down to answering four questions:

1. Where am I now?
2. Where am I going?
3. What is the path?
4. How do I keep moving?

If you answer those four questions with sincerity and a firm commitment, then you can create the result you want. Let's look at this in detail.

1. Where am I now?

A deceptively simple question that's often challenging to answer, especially if you're just learning to be honest.

If you have a phone with GPS in it, like most have these days, you can pull it out, open the map and see exactly where you are. Respecting personal or company goals, it may be more complicated.

For an income goal, pinpointing exactly where you are right now might be a challenge for you. You could face fear and may want to hedge the truth. You might want to leave out important details and circumstances that cause you to misstate the truth, even to yourself.

You might do this because of internal stories about being wrong. It may feel like a personal reflection of unworthiness. A lack of previous success might make it hard to admit precisely where we are.

Let's suppose you have always wanted to make your first million dollars. Today, your average income is $10,000 a month, which is somewhere around 10% of what you need. Rather than just being honest and factual, I often hear people say: "Well I'm gonna start this thing..."

Maybe you have a near-term plan to start an activity that you believe will generate cash and maybe you don't. That's not the point. The point is you have such embarrassment or other negative emotion around the truth that you clothe your answer in a future statement.

That is a hallmark of someone who is regularly dishonest. They use avoidance language as a security blanket as if directing attention to a future intention somehow reduces the negative impact of the actual present cash number.

If you want to get real with any achievement, then tell the truth. A foundation for all goals, especially if you're looking to achieve them quickly and with as few detours as possible, is to answer this question and all the rest that follow with the truth.

2. Where Am I Going?

This is another question that often seems very difficult to answer. As a coach, I regularly ask the question "What do you want?" At first, I was surprised at how much hesitation I heard. I'm no longer shocked that people can't tell me. I have heard it so often that it's more sad than shocking.

Fear of failure, fear of judgment and many other fears cloud the conversation. Whatever the reason, lack of clarity is not functional in creating progress toward a goal.

Just like the statement "I'm going to Kansas City," is inadequate because you don't know the address, vague goals without specifics are both difficult to reach and not very motivating.

The clearer the goal, the more details you have and the more certainty you feel about its importance, the easier it gets to achieve. The inclusion of a deadline also significantly increases the effectiveness of a statement about where you want to go.

3. What Is the Path?

Specifying the path to get from your present "Here," to the future "There," is a bit different. You often don't know the exact route you will take.

To answer this question, you might need to do some work to propose possible routes. There may be more than one way to get there.

You might do an opportunity and outcome analysis to pick the best path. However it's accomplished and whatever decision-making process you use to choose the way, it's something that must happen before you get very far out of the starting gate.

There are two reasons for this:

1. Wandering around, facing a general direction and hoping for a good outcome doesn't usually work. It also becomes frustrating and makes people want to quit.
2. No matter how well you plan, a fundamental truth about creating change and results is that your initial plan will be wrong. Sometimes a little and sometimes completely. That may suggest that planning is useless, but it's not. A rigorous planning process produces a starting point and information that will be useful when plans change.

As you create your intended path, you also need to figure out how you evaluate progress and make changes to your plan.

Experienced project managers have review and adjustment processes built into every plan they create.

Planning is different when you work for yourself, or you have a small company. In the section of the Results Equation™ titled "Courageous Plan," we will cover several methods to adapt planning to the solopreneur or small company.

4. How Do I Keep Moving?

One of the hallmarks of rigorous physical training is the mental aspect. For example, special operations forces such as Navy SEALs, spend as much time creating mental stamina as they do physical prowess, and with good reason.

There are lots of reasons we stop moving forward, and each requires a slightly different solution.

First, we may come to a place where we don't know what to do. We pause briefly to figure something out and get moving again. Effective planning includes knowing such delays happen and preparing for them by keeping your planning and action horizon far enough out to anticipate these times.

We may come to a point where we run out of resources. Obstacles may create unforeseen expenses, and you may run out of money. Again, this is something you plan for. A good plan includes a method to regroup, get more cash or trim the project.

Perhaps a needed part is delayed, or a city permit takes longer than promised or something needs redoing because it doesn't work as you expected. Anticipating those things and building in contingencies are Standard Operating Procedures for proper planning and project management.

All these obstacles have one thing in common. "Things happen." Circumstances change, stuff doesn't work out just right, and we make an accommodation. All these events can be anticipated and allowed for when creating a plan.

If the challenges and obstacles get big enough, then you take time to re-assess the purpose, the intended outcome, the deadlines, the resources, re-create the plan and start over.

Second, especially for those who work alone, own their own business or run a small company, there is a separate challenge. This challenge is the internal conversation on the stage of the mind.

Because the vision, the passion and the motivation all come from the business owner, a big reason you might stop moving is that you, as the big cog in the wheel, stop turning.

Something bad happens, and you lose motivation. You second guess yourself about the wisdom of this project. You get tired. You get lazy. You launch into stories of unworthiness. You know exactly what I mean. You can go from a powerhouse of achievement to a quivering mess in the space of an hour.

This internal dialogue is real and powerful. It cannot be mastered merely be screaming at yourself and saying, "suck it up!" All these dramas and stories are intangibles and have to do with the conversation between your ears.

It is difficult to accommodate all the variations of this struggle in a planning process. Instead, it would help if you had tools to quell the noise. Mastering these challenges to keep the momentum going requires a different skill set and a sharpened awareness.

A few examples:

- "I have no time to work on my business because I'm always working in my business."
- "I'm completely discouraged and out of balance."
- "I'll never get my head above water."
- "What if I'm just not cut out to do this."

These are typical expressions of someone who doesn't know how to manage the internal dialogue.

This "head trash" monster is responsible for the abandonment of more worthy and worthwhile efforts then all the rest of the barriers put together.

To satisfy this second reason we stop moving, we need something different than contingency plans, extra space in the timeline and extra cash.

Maintaining motivation and curing head trash are universally overlooked or downplayed precisely because of the lack of specificity of the problem. That doesn't make the consequences any less real or damaging. Ignoring this part will spell doom for your achievement.

The Results Equation was created to master all the challenges that come out of the four questions. If you follow the equation from start to finish, you can reach your goal, achieve the outcome you want and do a victory dance.

Part II

Creating the Equation

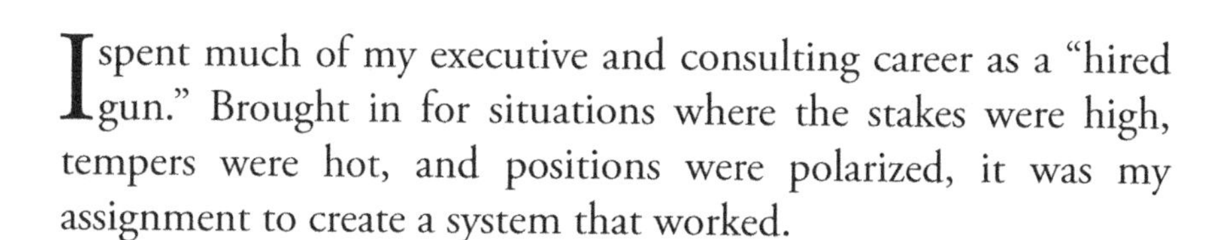

I spent much of my executive and consulting career as a "hired gun." Brought in for situations where the stakes were high, tempers were hot, and positions were polarized, it was my assignment to create a system that worked.

I didn't have the equation formulated during the years I did this work. I did what occurred to me by intuition. Each of us has natural gifts and talents, and one of my gifts is the ability to create "impossible" results in such situations.

When I retired from my consulting career, and I decided to coach, I knew that helping people "Do things they don't believe they can do," was exactly where I wanted to be.

Some coaches get trained in and follow a particular "system" for the work they do with clients. I explored many of these systems and found each one incomplete. The system might work well for a narrow application or particular situation but failed if the circumstance varied much from the script.

There is nothing "wrong" with such a system if the scope of work you do is narrow and fits the need. The range of consulting I had done gave me a larger field of vision about what was possible. I also realized that most systems completely ignore the complexities of the "head trash" portion of the problem.

What I saw happen over and over again is that coaches tried to cram a particular problem into the system they knew. That usually produced limited success and high levels of frustration.

If you get stuck on the idea that you have to cram the situation into the approach you know, it's like the old proverb, "if all you have is a hammer, then everything looks like a nail."

I created my own frameworks based on the commonalities I saw solving problems and getting results, regardless of the discipline or situation. I had plenty of source material from my decades of experience. I also researched methods used by other successful coaches, consultants and project managers.

As I coached, it became clear, just as I suspected, that there were striking similarities in getting to every result no matter what the problem was. That made sense to me since every achievement we want is just envisioning and then creating a change, or, moving from "Here" to "There."

The tools might vary, the environment is different, and the externalities will also be different. At heart, creating results is a simple process. After my research, I created an "equation" that encapsulates all the processes necessary to create any achievement.

When I went to university, I had a scholarship in mathematics, so I guess that's why I chose an "equation," to represent the journey. There is no math involved, but the idea of an equation represents predictability, certainty, and stability. All of these are characteristics of "The Results Equation™."

Part II has three sections. First, are three choices that you must make with an honest intention for success to come. Without certainty in these three choices, there will be delays and conflict. These choices determine your willingness to make something happen.

The Choices Are:

1. Planning vs. "Going with the Flow."
2. Deadlines vs. "When It Fits."
3. Prioritize vs. "One Among Many."

Second, are six principles describing the required personal characteristics. These characteristics must be present in each person on the project for maximum success. This is true for solopreneurs or each team member in a corporate goal. If these are not present or learned, there will be setbacks, careless mistakes, and endless procrastination.

The Principles Are:

1. Truth
2. Desire
3. Imagination
4. Optimism
5. Perseverance
6. Humility

These choices and principles create a context for success and help you quickly get to the heart of every question and challenge. They are the hallmarks of successful change and universal pitfalls if ignored.

Third, I will give the precise elements of The Results Equation™. This includes a description of each of the five steps in the equation, the reasons each is necessary and exercises to adapt it to your situation and complete the step successfully.

The Results Equation™ is:

UP + ME + CF + CP + RE = RESULTS

Chapter 20

Planning vs. "Going with the Flow"

This is the first of the three critical context choices.

Sometimes I get asked, "Isn't it too constraining to try to decide all this stuff ahead of time?" Put another way, "Since things change so much and so many unknowns exist, isn't it better just to get started than spend a lot of effort in planning?

Both these questions stem from a universal experience. Plans change, estimates are wrong, and externalities always interfere with what we're trying to do. That brings us to the question, "Since plans are never perfect, why the effort in creating a plan?"

Besides those questions, sometimes it feels great to make it up as you go along. If you're pursuing a hobby and don't care how long it takes or how many do-overs are required, then a haphazard approach may be perfectly suited to your project and temperament.

On the other hand, if the outcome and timing are essential, then a haphazard approach is full of pitfalls. This seems obvious, but I can't count the number of times I hear people say "I'll just get started and then we'll see what happens."

A vital element of any planning process is fundamental decisions about priorities, resources, timelines and other components required for a project.

A construction project is a great example. If you're building your own house and you have budgetary constraints, construction loan timelines, and sweat equity you will contribute, you must have a detailed schedule, especially if you have a full life besides the building project. To omit such a plan assures that one of your constraints will fail you.

After considering the variables, you may need a plan with an estimated completion range of somewhere between 24 and 36 months from now. As long as your cash reserve, financing deadlines and health allow it; this will work.

You must also factor in your willingness (and your family's tolerance) to live in a trailer or some reduced portion of the house while you deal with construction and the schedule adjustments. As long as you keep your enthusiasm high, you will eventually finish the project.

The Results Equation methodology would be ideal for the overall project. It would also be useful as the tool for each small section. This will become clear to you as the chapters unfold.

Most business decisions have tight timelines and performance demands. Shareholder expectations, management bonuses and market share might be on the line. When borrowing substantial money, your speed to market, emerging trends, seasonal shopping patterns and more, significantly impact your outcome.

A commitment to rigorous and thorough planning, with measurement and flexibility for change, is essential for success in any competitive market situation. Taking a solid plan into the equation process is a recipe for great success.

A dismal statistic we often hear is that a large majority of new businesses fail. Some studies suggest that at least 80% of businesses close in the first five years. The number is probably much higher since many start-up enterprises are never tracked.

My experience with start-ups and small businesses show me that fully 75% of these business failures could be avoided with good planning and the proper application of the Results Equation.

The first choice is a commitment to be decisive, rigorous and treat the planning process with the love and attention it deserves. In the next chapter, we'll discover how timelines fit into producing successful achievements.

Chapter 21

Deadlines vs. "When It Fits"

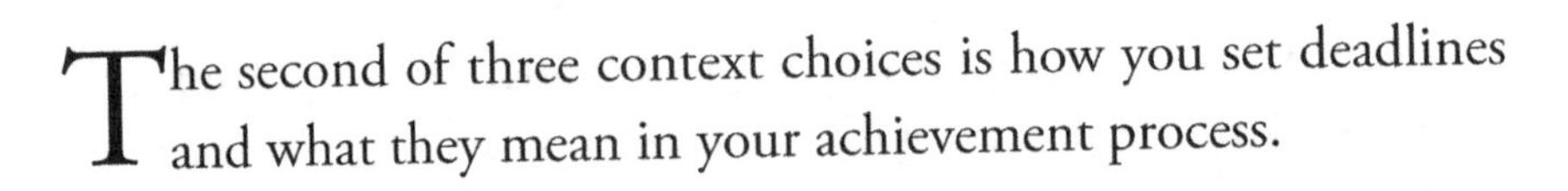

The second of three context choices is how you set deadlines and what they mean in your achievement process.

In my consulting career, I often entered a situation where there were high expectations and very tight deadlines. Sometimes the deadlines were imposed by legislation or other legal frameworks, and there was little to no flexibility.

Other times, deadlines were set arbitrarily with no real thought to the feasibility of reaching the goal in the time allotted.

For example, a person who says they are going to lose 50 pounds in the next month or two has a very high likelihood of failure. The declaration may come from a medical event like a failed health exam and is just a desperate reaction. Perhaps some less threatening but equally embarrassing spotlight drove the momentary bravado.

Regardless of the fierceness of the declaration or the firmness of the intent at the moment, creating unrealistic deadlines is almost always a deal killer.

That's not to say that you or I can't achieve seemingly ridiculous deadlines. You can. I have presided over intense projects where we met such deadlines. There are countless examples of this happening, and we don't hear about most of them.

In my experience, a deadline like can be a bit like a poison pill. If you meet the goal, it comes with casualties everywhere. Burnout, broken people and broken relationships are often the consequences. With the right preparation and framework, the project could get completed with an exhausted yet exultant team who have pulled together to create the "impossible" outcome.

How we present and interact with deadlines is a key determinant of the goal's success or failure. Why do deadlines exist? What do they mean? Are options for a deadline extension, if feasible, disclosed or explored? What incentives are available? What are the options for getting more help?

Deadlines and incentives are a vital part of any good project plan. This is no secret in successful business execution. How they are created and structured determines whether they will be successful as a motivator or feared as a consequence.

Clarity and buy-in are essential. In a group or company situation, this responsibility rests with the leader. How the leader presents the situation, how they act and talk about deadlines will determine the attitude of the team.

In an entrepreneurial situation, deadlines are usually arbitrary and ineffective. Someone just declares "we need to get this done by this date." Repeatedly, I see inadequate planning and no real understanding of the steps to get to the goal line, so it all feels like wishful thinking.

We act as if throwing the deadline in the air will cause us to find the time, energy and resources necessary to complete the project in a magical way yet to be invented.

Here are the key questions:

- Are there deadlines?
- What are the deadlines?
- What are the consequences of missing deadlines?
- Are there rewards or incentives for meeting the deadlines?
- Are there additional resources if timelines get tight?
- Are the deadlines arbitrary or connected in some way to a larger outcome?
- Is the leadership who created the deadlines committed to their achievement?
- As an entrepreneur, do you have a contingency plan if externalities derail your timeline?
- Do you have cash reserves to meet contingencies and stay on target?
- Have you done a reasonable analysis to determine whether the deadlines are feasible?
- And many other similar but nuanced questions.

The questions change depending on the project, but a sincere and honest relationship with deadlines involved in the project is required for success.

This is especially true for the solopreneur. When starting a new business, the owner wears ten hats. Creating additional stress from deadlines without good planning is counterproductive. At the same time, business success depends on meeting targets.

Deadlines are a way we keep score. If used to keep score and create incentives, they are far more likely to create results than if we treat them as punishment and a tool for embarrassment or criticism.

This is true in a corporate setting and a personal setting. In many cases, our own missed deadlines become objects of personal judgment and negativity.

This virtually guarantees abandonment of the project and failure. All of which is unnecessary if you handle deadlines correctly.

The Results Equation uses deadlines and incentives in a healthy and empowering way, and from this place drives more success and celebration.

Chapter 22

Prioritize vs. "One Among Many"

The last of the three context choices to prepare for success with "The Results Equation™," is a decision about how to prioritize the competing responsibilities you currently have.

You are already busy. You don't have much free time. Regularly, you may feel stressed to the breaking point, and the idea of adding more to your plate is scary.

Whenever you add something to your life, you must remove something else. For example, if you have decided to lose weight and get in shape, you must prioritize a current activity below your new work-out regime. This can be a temporary prioritization since you shouldn't be on a "weight loss" regime forever.

This is obvious, but at work and home, we keep telling ourselves we're going to do some "thing" and imagine the time to do it will present itself like magic. Consequently, it never happens.

The first step is to prioritize explicitly. Make a list of things that compete for your time. Specifically, declare which are a higher and lower priority than the new project. That way you can immediately get a picture of the likelihood of your success.

Estimate the daily or weekly time requirements of things that you declare to be a higher priority. You can quickly see what time you have left to start the new project moving.

If you prioritize most of your existing work and life responsibilities above the new project, expect that the timeline to finish it will be extensive. There is a high likelihood you'll get discouraged and quit unless you follow the steps in the equation.

An antidote to this discouragement is to declare your commitment. That is easy to say but sometimes scary to do. We often experience fear around such explicit vulnerability.

One reaction is to keep your declaration secret, so if you fail, no one knows. Another way is to get some accountability set up with a friend, a co-worker or a coach, so you have someone in your corner.

A problem with casual accountability is that your need may not be as important to the person you depend on. The support will likely be casual and intermittent. If the goal is important, you must carefully choose how to get dependable help.

Most of the time, making priorities get left to haphazard circumstance. This happens at work and at home. It occurs most regrettably with new business start-ups.

We hope we find time to do what we set out to do. We hope others understand when we change our regular availability or behavior. We waste time and energy hoping no one gets upset as we bumble along in a murky and unsatisfying haze.

Choosing to prioritize and then following through with priority setting, including conversations that flow from the decisions, is the critical hallmark of this choice.

Besides time allocation, we must also be explicit about the attitude, energy and focus you bring to the project. Whether driving a large corporate initiative or starting a business as an entrepreneur, how you direct your energy is critical to its success.

For example, let's consider an entrepreneurial startup since the illustrations are easiest to see and the omissions have the most obvious consequences.

It's important to note that the same decisions are necessary for a corporate project, a personal development goal or anything else. Look carefully, and you can see that by changing the words and making minor adaptations, this is universally true.

If you are a professional and you are looking to create a business on the side, then you have to answer the following questions about the energy required to make this happen:

- How many hours a week do I have to devote to this?
- What does my support system look like?
- How many months can I keep up a heavy work schedule which includes both my full-time job and the sideline I want to turn into a business.
- What are the ages of my kids and how can I manage those demands?
- How will I take care of myself physically and emotionally during this period of high stress?
- How much money do I have saved to pour into this project?

- What evidence do I have that this will work? Is it just a gut feeling, or am I entering the field with other successful market participants?
- How committed am I to make this happen?
- Is this something I genuinely want to do, or something someone else has encouraged or pushed me to try?
- And other similar questions.

Clearly understanding and declaring answers to these and related questions will help you make a good plan and create a successful outcome.

Again, this may seem obvious, but I can't tell you the number of people who can't answer these questions when they come seeking help from a business coach to make something successful.

If we don't explicitly assess readiness with our own list of questions, we are asking for trouble. When it bombs, it's easy to see why after the fact and we wonder why we didn't ask questions ahead of time.

Deliberately choosing and declaring the focus that the goal warrants is essential. If your focus is fuzzy, then momentary distractions will easily push aside what you planned.

For example, if you absolutely need to make the first few sales of a new product to have proof of concept, then that intense focus drives everything else to the back burner.

Setting the focus can be complicated. This isn't the only thing you are doing in your life or the only responsibility you have in your job.

If this is a work project and other departments are involved, this will include discussions among leadership teams. If you have a family and your new objective will change your schedule, and available time, you must have this conversation to gauge the buy-in.

Getting buy-in either at work or at home is just one element in creating success. It gives you a picture of the challenges you might face. It lets you see the sharks and pitfalls you need to navigate to make your way from “Here” to “There.”

Chapter 23

The Six Principles

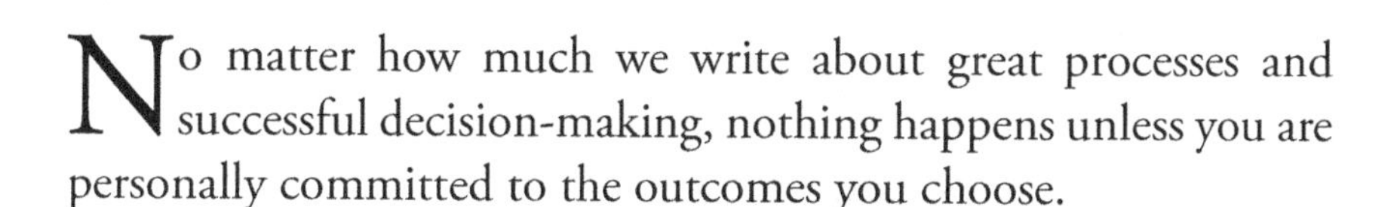

No matter how much we write about great processes and successful decision-making, nothing happens unless you are personally committed to the outcomes you choose.

A tentative wishing means that each decision along the way involves recommitment to the goal. If your decision at the start is firm, then a new decision is not required at each point along the way.

This chapter contains the six principles that are part of a Binding Internal Commitment. They are not optional. They are indispensable to successful change. They affect both the quality and speed of achieving goals you set or making changes you've chosen.

The Six Principles for Results are:

1. Truth
2. Desire
3. Imagination
4. Optimism
5. Perseverance
6. Humility

Principle #1 – Truth

I put this first because it is the bedrock foundation of everything else. It may seem self-evident that living in truth is essential to proper goal setting and achievement, but, it's not and it's not practiced.

I am continually blown away by people unwilling to be truthful about many aspects of change. This comes primarily from an unwillingness to see things as they are.

If you start this section already squirming in your chair, then you know what I mean. The squirming means you live in a grey place full of "maybe" or "that depends."

There are lots of reasons for this. Some are accustomed to seeing what they want to see. Taking off the filtered glasses is a painful exercise.

Some view the absolute truth as an enemy which we must avoid at all costs. Perhaps they associate truth with some form of judgment about "good or bad."

Some believe that "truth is in the eye of the beholder." While this may be with politics or social views, it isn't beneficial when setting goals either as an individual or member of a team.

To make this as simple as possible let's define truth as:

- An accurate representation of facts surrounding the goal you wish to achieve.
- An unflinching assessment of what you've already done. A statement of what you are willing to do to accomplish the goal.

Often "telling the truth" is associated with an admission of failure or weakness. That view makes people reluctant because it can feel like an exposure of vulnerability or validation of a story that they are "not good enough."

If we drop the drama and define truth as necessary facts and statements about where we are, where we're going, how to get there and how to keep moving, then we can avoid the internal churning and "head trash" associated with telling the truth.

Principle #2 – Desire

What is it that you want to achieve? I am continually surprised at the difficulty, and lack of precision people show when I ask, "What do you want?"

Desire comes when the goal is something *you* want. Sometimes, we set goals because we are "supposed to" do a certain thing, be a certain way or reach certain milestones.

It's possible to achieve a goal from someone else's agenda, and it happens all the time. The most effective and fastest way to get your goals accomplished is to separate those that spring from your well of creativity from those that are obligations you adopted from someone else's script.

What is the source of the goal? Why do you want it? How long have you wanted it? Can you imagine your life if you never achieve this goal? Does this goal matter to anyone else?

These and similar questions can help to sort out the real reason you want a goal. If you have a clear sense the goal is something you want, and you know why it's important, this knowledge will move mountains in staying motivated and doing what's required when the path gets steep.

Principle #3 – Imagination

No matter how you first picture the road from where you are to the goal you want, it will be filled with twists, turns, and unexpected setbacks. Imagination is the key to facing challenges and obstacles that show up along the way.

Imagination is the foundation of all great achievement. Regularly spending time in a state of imagination keeps the goal present and powerful and leads to creativity in accomplishing the objective.

Your ability to keep the goal conceptualized in your mind, and imagine different roads to get there, is foundational to staying in motion on the path until you're done.

You must be willing to imagine beyond the immediate tasks in front of you and feel connected to the great opportunities and successes you're not yet able to see.

Principle #4 – Optimism

You may wonder why optimism is a critical characteristic of a person who accomplishes goals. Decades of study by Dr. Martin Seligman have incontrovertibly demonstrated those who hold an optimistic view of life make more money, achieve more goals, perform better both on and off the playing field and in the boardroom. Optimism is a key ingredient for high performance.

Also, they live longer, have more inner happiness and seem to have more fun. Who wouldn't want that? The good news is optimism is a choice, not something you're born with. Whenever obstacles occur, and they will, choosing to view the situation optimistically increases the speed and flexibility of the solutions.

An optimist believes a solution can be found and sets out to work immediately figuring out how to get it done instead of wasting time wondering whether the whole project is a bust.

You may start a project optimistically and then get bogged down in the middle and want to quit. Temporary setbacks and frustration are normal, and it is a rule of life that everything takes longer than we think it does.

Optimism is not a one-time event. Even with temporary setbacks and frustration, the optimist thinks there is a way, that the effort to find it is necessary and they will be amply rewarded at the goal line.

Principle #5 – Perseverance

Every goal will encounter pitfalls and slowdowns. Perseverance is the quality of continuing to move forward in the face of opposition, setbacks, naysayers and other barriers to progress.

Problems not foreseen at the beginning will show up and make the way harder than you thought. Perseverance in such situations yields unexpected results and rewards also not anticipated.

Perseverance is a quality we unabashedly admire when the Olympian running a race falls, gets scratched up, jumps up and finishes the race. If somehow, they find the grit and determination to win or place, such is the stuff of legend.

While your perseverance and victories may not make headline news, a choice to persevere in the face of difficulty forever changes the nature of your soul. It gives you insight and courage where others would see trouble and fear.

Perseverance is the glue that holds everything together. Without it, regardless of your vision, imagination, and enthusiasm, the goal remains a wish, and you forever wonder "What if I had just kept going?"

Principle #6 – Humility

Humility may sound like a strange characteristic to be in the list of required qualities for achievement. It comes from the truth that no significant objectives were ever achieved alone.

Humility means you're smart enough and have enough wisdom to get the needed help. Getting lost is easy; staying lost when people around you can provide directions is stupid.

A willingness to be taught, be open to learning and to change your mind in the face of useful information cannot be overvalued as a characteristic of success.

Humility is not being a doormat and laying down because of the will or determination of someone else. Humility is a strength; it demonstrates wisdom and provides a powerful platform for every goal you ever hope to accomplish.

These six principles form a solid foundation and give you the vision, courage, and steadiness to accomplish even difficult objectives.

Whether the goal you have is intensely personal and is a change to your principal character or habits, or you're involved in a corporate goal that requires teamwork, cash investment and ground-breaking changes in your industry, these principles are the bedrock of the high achiever.

Chapter 24

The Equation

The Results Equation™ isn't long, and it's not complicated. It consists of five steps that allow you to conceptualize and execute a strategy to get from "Here" to "There."

This is the results equation:

UP + ME + CF + CP + RE = Results

In chapter 18 I talked about four questions required to get a project finished. The "Results Equation™ is a formal representation of these four questions and splits one of them into two parts.

UP is Understanding the Present. The present is the existing set of conditions. If you are traveling, it's the precise location where you are now.

"Understanding the Present," is not just truthfully expressing facts about the present but also understanding what they mean for the future.

ME is Mental Earthquake. An earthquake is a shakeup. Tectonic plates below the earth's surface create pressure through the movement of magma underneath. Eventually, they slip and grind and cause shock waves through the earth.

Shock waves in our mental makeup and what we believe is possible is often required to achieve goals. If goals were easy, we'd complete them all, and there wouldn't be any struggle in making them real.

We make empty promises all of the time. We set New Year's resolutions; corporate goals are established and often, failure is the rule, not the exception.

The Mental Earthquake is the mental half of the question, "How do I keep moving?"

CF is Creating the Future. One of the four questions is "Where am I going?" It's easy to give a vague description about where you're going like "I want to be rich."

We know from experience that accomplishes nothing, and such statements are little more than a pipe dream. Creating the future is a process of declaring and describing an outcome so vividly that the vision itself becomes a motivator.

A goal statement is nothing without specifics. Details, feelings, and reasons associated with the accomplishment of the goal become are part of the fabric. Creating the future is a goalsetting process unlike any other.

CP is Courageous Planning. It is easy to avoid planning or to slapdash something together. What makes some plans effective and others little more than marks on a piece of paper?

Courageous planning involves an element of risk. It involves planning that pushes the envelope while at the same time remaining grounded enough, in reality, to keep motivation high.

It also involves a realistic assessment of the time, energy and resources required to accomplish a given objective. This part is often overlooked, especially in the world of small business and the solopreneur.

RE is relentless execution. This is the other half of the question "How do I keep moving?" The word relentless means to continue in the face of opposition or obstacles.

Mindless action, however furious, rarely results in coherent progress. This means that execution must be directional, focused and continuous.

How do we stay on schedule? How do we behave in the face of setbacks? How do we adjust the plan when things go completely off the rails? Relentless execution is the key.

Chapter 25

Choosing the Result

The results that you wish to achieve can be any size. For those new to the Results Equation, start first with something achievable in 90 days or less. The equation works with anything, but longer-term goals are more complicated than shorter ones.

Even though the results equation works with all objectives, until you have some experience, it can feel daunting if you start with something big. Besides, 90 days pass quickly, so, the reward of achieving a short-term goal will be sweet.

If you have something gigantic in mind, break it down. Start with a chunk that, though challenging, can be done in 90 days. You will successfully create your first result and be familiar with the method.

Let me repeat this. It works best for beginners to use something achievable in 90 days or less.

When picking the result, it must be precise. There can be no question about why you want it and exactly what it looks and feels like.

Describe the result in a way that someone else can understand. Here are some simple examples, but you'll want to create one of your own.

- "I want to lose weight" versus "I want to lose 30 pounds in 90 days."
- "I want to make more money" versus "I want to increase my income to an average of $10,000 per month from my current average of $5,000 per month, in 90 days." "I want to write a book" versus "I want to have a book finished and published in 90 days."
- "I want a better relationship" versus "I want to have my partner express gratitude for the growth in our relationship at least four times in 90 days."
- "I want to get off drugs" versus "I want to have 89 days of sobriety in 90 days."

If you can't describe the goal in precise terms, you will not know when you have achieved it, and milestones will be fuzzy. This leads to cheating and failure.

This is especially true with goals that involve feelings or perceptions. Ninety days from today it will be impossible for us to remember exactly what we feel like today.

Memory is reconstructive, and how we remember today will be drastically influenced by what happens between now and the time you "remember."

Specifying a clear, unambiguous result that can be understood by someone else is the non-negotiable essential for starting the Results Equation.

Define your results here:

____

____

____

____

____

____

____

The very nature of accomplishing difficult things requires iteration at every step of the process. Iteration is the heart and soul of a successful application. It's expected that you'll write several versions before you settle on one.

You may even revisit the goal partway through the process. Discoveries and circumstances may suggest or require such a change. As long as truth is the guide and you are not cheating yourself, that's fine.

Don't be discouraged. Exercise your creativity, invest in yourself by hiring a coach, create awesome results, and celebrate your successes in a way that encourages your heart and makes your life magnificent.

Chapter 26

UP = Understanding the Present

Every term in the "Results Equation ™" has a fundamental purpose. The purpose of UP is to learn to know the truth, tell the truth and be comfortable with the truth.

The best way to think about the equation is to compare it to a journey. "You are where you are," and "it is what it is." However irritating these phrases may seem, they are the foundational truth of all change.

You cannot start a journey from somewhere you're not or pretending that you are something that you're not. So of course, the first term in the results equation is "UP" for *Understanding the Present.*

This may seem ridiculously simple, but it isn't. Often it is the most difficult part. That's because of the struggle we have with the truth.

We are *unwilling,* to tell the truth, in all of its naked glory, about where we are, what we have, what we're doing and what is required to get what we want.

This habit comes from various places: fear of judgment, fear of failure, fear of being inadequate and many other things from the past. If you feel that, it's normal, and you're not alone. You can learn a new way of being and overcome this barrier to growth.

If the truth has been hard for you, or you have a habit of only being partially honest, then this step will be particularly challenging. As we go through this, I will continually refer to the "TRUTH." We are not discussing religious doctrine, universal truth or the mysteries of the universe.

The results equation starts with the truth about your present situation concerning the goal you've set. This will serve as a foundation for achievement. You will remember that the first of six principles for success is an absolute commitment to telling the truth.

In this case, it's a set of facts. It does not include a bunch of judgment or emotion or anger or blame, as these things do not effectively contribute to the journey. So drop the drama about your past performance and capability.

The "UP" portion of the equation consists of six questions. Remember that starting on this journey assumes you already specified the precise result you want by completing the assignment in Chapter 25. If you haven't done that exercise, stop reading, and go back and complete it. Make sure you come to this step with a clear and measurable outcome.

Question 1 – Where Am I?

The answer to this question is expressed in the same terms you use to define the *result* you want. For example: if the result is "I want to lose 30 pounds in the next four months," then the "where am I?" question is answered with a simple number.

Include today's date and the relevant measure. For example: "Today is June 1st, and my weight is 210 pounds." No excuses, no explanations – just the answer.

If your result is more complicated, then the answer will be more involved.

For example, if your goal is "I want my average monthly income to be $10,000 a month, six months from today," then the answer to "Where am I now?" could be "Today is June 1st and my average monthly income is $5,000.

One place to check the truth is how you create the average in this example. If you recently had a large sale, then it may distort the average, and that won't help you achieve your goal. Look back over an appropriate period, exclude any extraordinary events, and create an average that's meaningful.

I can't overemphasize the significance of this step. We often gloss over precision and avoid specifics. You are not trying to impress anyone, and you know when you are cheating.

If you have a job with a salary, then your income number is easy. You may be thinking of a promotion or creating a side business to achieve the increase. If you already have a business, and like most entrepreneurs, your income varies, then you're going to have to do some calculating.

Remember, it would be easy to cheat, and if you do, you are cheating yourself of the benefit of the equation process.

Question 2 – How did I get here?

This question requires even more of the truth than the first one.

This is not designed to create a field day for excuses, blame, anger, frustration or any other emotions that cloud the process. The correct answer is a simple acknowledgment of the series of choices you made which landed you in the spot you're in now.

Back to our example of weight, the answer could be a simple list:

1. I don't exercise regularly.
2. I have poor nutritional habits.
3. I snack late at night.
4. I'm an emotional eater and eat for comfort.

It is essential to be thorough, so you don't leave out critical pieces. If you want a new result, then you need a new system, and you can't create one if you don't understand the system you have now. Remember, truth is essential.

If you make a good list of how you got here, you will have all the pieces needed for moving forward with the next question and the full process. In saying this, I want to add a caution to avoid wasting time trying to be "perfect." Be honest, be complete and then be done.

Question 3 – Why am I not moving, or moving fast enough toward my goal?

This question may sound the same as the last one, but there are significant differences. The previous question focuses on specific choices and behaviors that got you where you are now. This question deals more with examining attitudes and beliefs that may need adjustment.

If you continue the behaviors that got you where you are, you will stay where you are. The beliefs and stories you have about changing those behaviors are important. This becomes critical when you set a new goal, or you recommit to a goal you've had before. Truth is essential.

For example, you may believe that change isn't possible. You may believe that success isn't your destiny. You may feel that you are somehow "not good enough." You may feel you do not have the tools or knowledge to move forward.

That list is quite different from the behaviors that got you where you are. Answer this question carefully and discover what is impeding the changes needed for your trip from "Here" to "There."

Question 4 – What behaviors, habits and attitudes need to change for me to start making progress?

The answer to this question will come from combining what you wrote for questions two and three. You will be tempted to shortcut this and say "I know what I have to do." Give the process a little time, write it down and be complete. Your reward will come later.

It is not necessary, or wise, to list every single habit, belief or behavior that would optimize maximum performance. That is overwhelming and a sure way to quit before you start. The pursuit of perfection is the fastest way to ensure you do nothing. Instead, begin with a short list.

List no more than five habits or beliefs that must change for you to begin to make progress. The number of things you need will depend on your goal, and the answers to question two and three above.

Make sure the list is complete enough, so you are confident that if you make the changes listed, you will begin to make progress at a speed that is satisfactory to your heart and desire.

Pace matters. If the movement feels too slow or seems unnoticeable, you'll get frustrated and quit. If you try to do everything, you'll be overwhelmed and stall.

Question 5 – What is the first small thing I can do today that begins the process of change?

Creating an immediate step and a commitment to do it today is the fastest way to get started.

Don't spend a lot of time thinking about it. Instead, pick an obvious small change that you're willing to make right now and begin the process of progress.

There are a couple of reasons for this:

- Success breeds success. Having one thing started will encourage you to do another.

- The journey of a thousand miles begins with one step, and now you only have 999 left to take.

Question 6 - What accountability process will I set up to ensure I take all the required action?

It won't matter how good the answers to the questions are or how fast you take the first step if you don't have an accountability process. Change can be difficult and the bigger the change, the harder it seems.

Even though you create immediate success by completing question five, you will need to take all the steps to get to the goal line. External accountability is a proven method to help sustain momentum.

There are many accountability processes. The most obvious and most successful is to hire a coach who understands your goals and will hold you accountable in a powerful and encouraging way. This is the sure-fire way used by top performers in athletics, business, performing arts and in life itself.

If you choose not to hire a coach, then an accountability partner, a business associate, or someone who cares about your progress is the next best option.

You must have someone who will hold you accountable fairly and firmly, and not someone who will accept excuses and nonsense as reasons for non-performance. Choose carefully and if your first choice doesn't work out, pick a different one.

Below is space for you to complete the six questions for your own goal. The best way to understand the Results Equation is to put it into action.

If you give yourself the gift of truth and some time to complete the exercise, you will feel opportunity blossoming before your eyes. You will have a specific goal and an accurate assessment of where you are, how you got here, and what needs to change.

Most encouragingly, you will be committed to the first small step towards victory.

Copy your Result from Chapter 25

____

____

____

____

____

____

____

____

____

____

____

____

Where Are You?

How Did You Get Here?

Why Are You Not Moving? (or, not moving fast enough?)

What Habits, Choices, Behaviors and Beliefs Need to Change For You To Move?

What is the First Small Step You Commit to Do TODAY?

What Is the Accountability Process You Will Use to Ensure Success?

Go through your answers a few times. The very nature of accomplishing difficult things requires iteration in every step of the process. Repetition is the heart and soul of successful growth.

Don't be discouraged. Exercise your creativity, invest in yourself by hiring a coach, create awesome results, and celebrate your successes.

Chapter 27

ME = Mental Earthquake

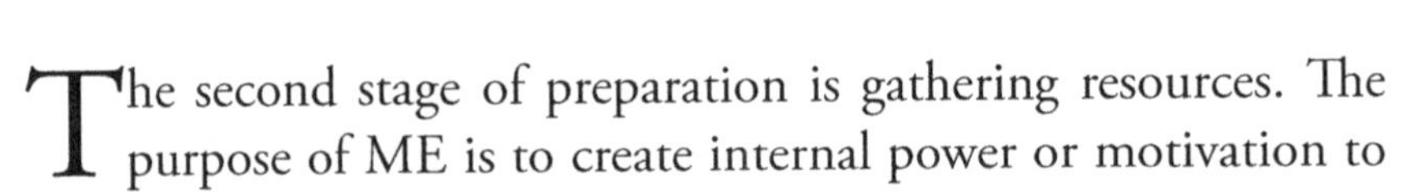

The second stage of preparation is gathering resources. The purpose of ME is to create internal power or motivation to keep moving.

After the UP module, you understand precisely where you are, how you got there, why you haven't been moving, and you listed things that need to change to get you moving in the right direction. You also took the first steps toward the goal.

This module focuses on creating the power you need to make and sustain those changes. In Chapter 24, I said that mental earthquake was half the answer to the question "How do I keep moving?"

In many ways, the internal game is more important and difficult than learning the external steps needed to accomplish a goal. That's why it comes now in the equation.

Habits, practices, attitudes, and beliefs are powerful. They can either move you purposefully in the right direction or hold you back in a sturdy grip.

Habits make wonderful servants and terrible masters. Your habits, practices, attitudes, and beliefs have served you, and create your existence today. When you decide you want a *new* level of performance, you have to develop new habits, practices, attitudes, and beliefs.

This doesn't mean everything changes. You identify and change those habits, practices, attitudes, and beliefs that no longer serve you. How do you create the internal resolve to change these parts of yourself that need to grow?

To make it easy, let's break it into small steps. Usually, if we want to change something in ourselves, the first place we look is outside us. As a rule, we fear change and start from the belief we don't have what it takes, so we must go get it.

For example:

- We look for a new book.
- We look for a new online course.
- We look for a new teacher.
- We look for a new tool.
- We look for some great epiphany.
- And on and on.

No doubt all these things are valuable and contain great information and tools, but they do not create the power we need to change.

We look outside because we don't trust ourselves, we don't believe we are strong enough, we have failed in the past, or for dozens of other reasons that may be personal and private.

We may know the reasons, or they may be hidden in our subconscious mind.

In other words, we believe we have little power. We certainly don't have enough power to change habits, practices, attitudes, and beliefs that are keeping us from our goals.

The fact that we don't trust ourselves or don't believe that we are adequate or "good enough," fundamentally comes from a lack of self-love.

It may be hidden with a hundred other labels, but the missing key is self-love. In my case, I lived with the story of "not good enough," from decades of depression. I finally understood the causes and acted to fix it.

One step I took was to write my story in *Tightrope of Depression*. If you want to know more about this book, the details are in the Appendix.

Regardless of the cause, our lack of confidence and low opinion of our abilities stems from accepting external messages that all point to "you can't cut it."

That is the most pervasive and poisonous sentiment in the world. Learning to love yourself and accepting the truth that you *are* enough, is the foundation of all power to create results for yourself.

To create and sustain power to change internal stories and habits, practices, attitudes and beliefs that go with them, we must start with self-love.

The good news is that self-love is your natural state. You started life accepting yourself as you were and only learned later that somehow you were "weak" or flawed." Learning to love yourself is dumping baggage that you don't need, is not true and you didn't have to start with.

Two Powerful Exercises

There are two simple and powerful exercises that I use and teach coaching clients to start an immediate positive change to your self-love framework:

First, every day for five minutes, look in the mirror and proclaim sincerely and truthfully, "I Love You."

This may be awkward at first but do it anyway, for five minutes *every* day. This is not a habit you do for a little while. It's a habit that you start now and do for the rest of your life.

Over years of coaching, I have noticed a couple of fascinating things. First, the harder this exercise is to start with, the more you need to grow your self-love. Second, the longer you do it, the easier it gets and the more powerful the result.

This book doesn't go into the full explanation of why this works. If you want more detail about why this is so powerful and necessary, you can read *Meeting God at the Door.* Details are in the Appendix.

What I can tell you for sure is that if you do this every day, your confidence to change will increase dramatically. Your power to stay committed will grow exponentially. Challenges that were hard for you will become easier.

Over the years, I have seen this result repeatedly in my coaching practice and significant ways in my own life.

The second exercise is a more in-depth exploration of what it means to love yourself. It's a practice of declaring certain truths in a compelling way, that reminds you who you are and what you are about, as you make changes and create new achievements.

Repeating phrases to yourself is sometimes called "saying affirmations" in the self-help world. I want to draw a clear distinction between simply "saying affirmations" and declaring true things.

An affirmation is often a statement that you don't believe but want to believe. Or, it can be a statement you think you should believe and that others have told you is true. You hope by continued repetition to make yourself believe it.

I am not finding fault with any use of affirmations. My experience teaches they are a weak cousin of the declaration process embodied in the second exercise.

The declarations that I use are below.

- I am Loved
- I am Worthy
- I am Grateful
- I am Happy
- I am Clear
- I am Committed
- I am Useful

There are three keys to making the process of declaration work for you.

1. Speak one declaration out loud, slowly and clearly. Repetition is not the key.

2. Take time to experience the meaning of each word. For example, "I Am Loved," has three words and each has significance.

   "I" denotes the essence of your being, not the physical body. The conscious entity that you are is speaking the truth and at the same time acknowledging the experience.

   "AM" is a present tense verb. It denotes an existing situation. You are in fact at this moment loved. By God, by others in your world and hopefully by yourself.

   "LOVED" is a statement and acknowledgment about a condition of caring, concern, yearning and nurturing. Those who love you, do so without your permission or consent.

3. Think in your mind and then feel in your body the experience of being loved, cherished, precious and of great importance to those who love you. Allow this experience to penetrate each cell in your body so that you know and feel the truth of that love.

Using this practice, speak each declaration and take whatever time is necessary so that the experience penetrates your body and your emotional context.

In this way, the declarations become a statement of your truth and not an articulation of a wish or an attempt to convince yourself of the truth of something you doubt.

If the declarations I use are not something you can do in this fashion, then create your own. They must motivate you, resonate with you and creative vibrancy and power or they're not the right declarations for you. Experiment until they cause you to tremble with excitement and certainty.

The practice of speaking declarations should begin while you are still doing the UP (Understanding the Present) module. It is essential that they become a habit and start creating power for you as you create your own "Mental Earthquake."

The "Mental Earthquake" is the description of what happens in your mind and your heart when you realize that you have access to all the power you need to make any change you want. You can quit any habit, start a new habit, reach any result, and create any outcome you wish.

The biggest barrier is simply the fact that you don't believe that it's so.

The two key principles in this module are captured in two statements that are also written as acronyms.

The first teaches a truth that, while external resources are valuable and motivating, the true power lies within you and can be activated as described above. To remember this truth I use this equation:

TPI^2Y = The Power Is In You.

After you internalize the truth that the power resides in you and is not "out there" somewhere, the second key is to learn that you can make it available anytime you want. I call this: "Learning to make your power rock." It's represented in the following statement:

ROC = Rumble On Command.

Let's talk first about accepting the truth that we have the power we need already inside of us. There are two big reasons we rob ourselves of our power.

First, we don't truly believe in ourselves. Sometimes we describe this as low self-esteem. It has a thousand names and a thousand descriptions. They all come down to some version of "I'm not good enough," so we don't believe we are worthy of good things.

Second, we perceive change as painful and want to avoid it at all costs. Making a personal change is the thing that people avoid more than anything else in the world. We become comfortable with how things are, even if they're not pleasant. The unknown nature of change creates even more fear.

The declarations described above are the beginnings of creating self-love. Achieving small wins by setting small goals, and then keeping promises, increases our confidence and ability to do more.

This is why accountability for the small steps you started in the "UP" module is so critical. You must begin to keep your promises. Then you must set up an accountability and feedback system so that you keep *more* promises, and eventually keep *all* your promises.

Here are some questions to help you with the first principle. Answering these truthfully will anchor the truth that the power is in you (TPI^{2}Y). Remember, repetition is key to learning and success.

Do I love myself? ______________________________

What specifically about my behavior proves this is true?

____

____

____

____

____

____

____

Do I trust myself? ______________________________

What specifically about my behavior proves this is true?

____

____

____

____

____

____

____

Am I caring for myself? ___________________________

What specifically about my behavior proves this is true?

____

____

____

____

____

____

____

Now let's talk about how to make this power ROC, or "Rumble on Command."

Making your power rumble on command describes your ability to call the power you have into any situation and make it work for you. This is especially important when facing challenges, discouragement, or distractions.

There is no magic wand. Just like any other skill, the only way to make your power "rumble on command," is practice. To help with this practice, I've created some things that I personally use and use with clients.

Most things that keep us from accessing our power can be categorized into three areas:

Distractions – things that we do that are fun, interesting and time wasting. We do them either because we can, or as an excuse *not* to do the important things. Many things which seem "urgent" but are not actually "important," fall into this category.

Deflections – excuses we make about why something is not our fault, or explanations and rationalizations about how we've done everything we can, and there's nothing more to do. We manifest this verbal manipulation either to ourselves or others to avoid the "guilt" associated with not keeping commitments.

Discouragement – how we feel when things fail, we have big detours or stuff seems overwhelming. We give up momentarily or put things off until "later." Eventually, we quit entirely, or something kicks us in the rear end, and we get moving again.

The process of making our power "rumble on command" is simple, but sometimes tricky. This is because it involves telling the truth about our intentions, our excuses, and our motivation to make something happen. Here is a practice I use:

- First, identify your Distractions, Deflections, and Discouragements.
- Second, for one of these, create a new commitment about what to do when that situation or feeling comes up.
- Third, write the commitment down as an action you take to keep moving in the direction of your goal.

There are many ways to do this and lots of self-help material focused on how we make choices and keep commitments. The best way to get this done effectively is to hire a coach, so you have someone in your corner.

I have four distinctions that I use with myself and clients that help me as I go through this process.

Pretend vs. Reality – We love to pretend and tell ourselves stories about what's going on, instead of telling the truth. Slowing down enough to assess the truth of the obstacle or distraction and then acting on the answer is the key.

Avoid vs. Experience – We shy away from things we perceive as difficult even if we suspect the experience would benefit our growth. Consciously choosing to have a growth experience removes fear and enhances skills and confidence.

Tolerate vs. Embrace – We put up with things we feel are unacceptable or unpleasant because we're too lazy or too frightened to change them. This shows up in relationships, health issues like weight or smoking or in accepting things because "that's just the way things are." If we come from the place of "ownership" instead of "victimhood," we can fully accept and embrace a situation, or create a plan for change. The key is in the decision.

Weakened vs. Empowered – Every challenging circumstance leaves us either weakened or empowered. Often the difference comes from attitude. Seeing things as happening "for us" instead of "to us" is a mindset that allows a challenge to create power instead of resignation.

EXERCISE

In the space below, write your own Distractions, Deflections, and Discouragements. Explicitly commit to actions you will take in each situation so you will have the power to create the outcome you want. Use the distinctions above as appropriate to help with this exercise.

Describe a Distraction, Deflection or Discouragement:

____

____

____

____

____

____

State Your Commitment to Change that Supports Your Result:

____

____

____

____

____

____

____

____

Distraction, Deflection or Discouragement #2:

State Your Commitment to Change that Supports Your Result:

Distraction, Deflection or Discouragement #3:

State Your Commitment to Change that Supports Your Result:

Distraction, Deflection or Discouragement #4:

State Your Commitment to Change that Supports Your Result:

Distraction, Deflection or Discouragement #5:

State Your Commitment to Change that Supports Your Result:

Distraction, Deflection or Discouragement #6:

State Your Commitment to Change that Supports Your Result:

____

____

____

____

____

____

Distraction, Deflection or Discouragement #7:

____

____

____

____

____

____

State Your Commitment to Change that Supports Your Result:

____

____

____

____

____

____

____

Distraction, Deflection or Discouragement #8:

____

____

____

____

____

____

State Your Commitment to Change that Supports Your Result:

____

____

____

____

____

____

There is no exact "right" or "wrong" way to do this. Just get started and allow the process to unfold for you. Remember, the nature of accomplishing difficult things requires iteration at each step of the process. Practice is the heart and soul of successful growth.

Above all, don't be discouraged. Exercise your creativity, invest in yourself by hiring a coach. Enjoy discovering your real inner power.

Chapter 28

CF = Create the Future

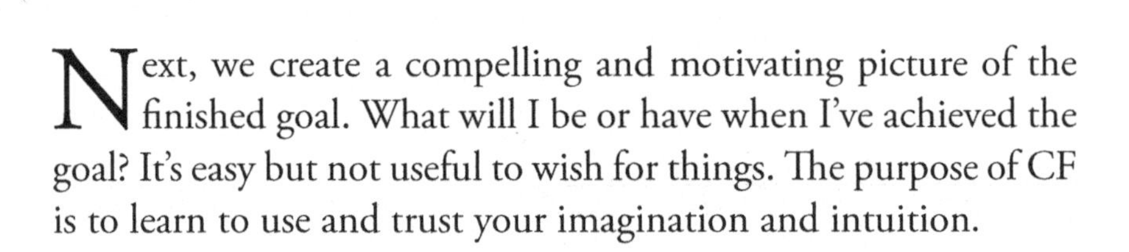

Next, we create a compelling and motivating picture of the finished goal. What will I be or have when I've achieved the goal? It's easy but not useful to wish for things. The purpose of CF is to learn to use and trust your imagination and intuition.

This section starts with a simple premise: "You Can't Create What You Can't Imagine."

The "Results Equation" works for any result you want to create. Often, I get asked "How detailed does each step of the equation need to be?

The answer is simple. How certain are you that the goal you set will happen? Are you certain you will achieve the result, simply, effectively, and in a timely fashion? If the answer is, "yes," then no complexity is required.

Instead, if the goal seems daunting, or you have already tried multiple times to get a result, repeatedly failed, chosen procrastination over progress, and find yourself frustrated or at a loss about how to get from "Here" to "There," then apply the equation.

In this section, which builds on understanding where you are and stoking the fire of your desire, you will create a clear and specific future state that represents the result you're committed to.

Often, we confuse the dynamic process of "Creating the Future" with daydreaming, wishful thinking, creating a vision board, making New Year's resolutions and other shallow placebos.

We love telling ourselves stories about what the future might look like if our wish list came true. At the same time, we know in our hearts it won't happen, because we're not doing anything about it.

"Creating the Future," is the process of building the image of a future state in such a powerful way that it perpetually fires the drive to make it real.

There are three parts to creating that powerful future:

- See an Inspiring Vision.
- Feel a Motivating Intention.
- Declare your Total Commitment.

See an Inspiring Vision

We all daydream – we see a big house or a nice car and want it. We all look at others' lives and imagine that they're so fantastic that we would like to have them.

The effectiveness of your "Inspiring Vision" depends first on its completeness. A vague idea is not inspirational.

A clear and precise picture has all the details that give life; colors, sizes, background, and sounds are necessary to create a crystal clear and compelling vision.

In the context of the achievement you want, you must know *exactly* what success looks like. Some examples:

- You must know how many zeros are in your bank account when you declare the result you wish to achieve.
- You must know what your partner will say or do to demonstrate the level of intimacy and connectedness that defines the success you seek.
- You must have a precise goal for your health; including weight, blood pressure, heart rate, and related metrics so that the achievement is complete and meaningful.

Many dreams have failed due to this lack of specificity. For example, you specify an income amount. You don't pinpoint where in the revenue chain that number comes from.

You achieve that number in gross sales, but expenses are so high, your net number is smaller than your current take-home.

Not what you meant, right? It would help if you had all the appropriate parameters for an income target to be meaningful and powerful.

Results are as varied as the people who want them, so I can't tell you exactly how to do this. Here are some ideas that have proven helpful in creating an "Inspiring Vision."

- Be clear.
- Be specific.
- Be outrageous.
- Be truthful.
- Have fun.
- Let it flow.
- Don't worry about the "how."
- Don't ask permission.

If a goal seems outrageous, or the vision you see seems excessive, ask a simple question: "Why Not?" Another helpful question is to continue asking yourself, "What Else?" Do it until you run out of things to say.

The process of letting your imagination run free, *including* describing all the necessary details, helps to free your mind from preconceived notions about what is possible from your current viewpoint.

It is far easier to trim an excessively ambitious goal than it is to create a goal conceived in fear and a context of limited beliefs.

Looking up at a high mountain from the valley below is nowhere near as inspiring as standing on the peak and looking at the view. Since this phase of the equation is conducted in the imagination, why stand in the valley instead of on the mountaintop?

For the achievement you have committed to, list the specific details in the space below. This includes the sights, sounds, colors, smells and everything else that will be there when you achieve this result.

List the Details Here:

____

____

____

____

____

____

____

____

____

____

Read it out loud a half-dozen times. How does it feel? Does speaking the vision give you goosebumps? Does it create a yearning in your soul? Does it make you breathe faster and make your heart race?

If these feelings are not present, the vision is too small, you don't have enough detail, or it isn't something you really want. If that's where you are, re-examine the result, the details you've described, and your expression of the achievement until you have a vision of your future that takes your breath away every time you think about it.

Feel A Motivating Intention

One source of power in "Creating the Future," is the *feeling* associated with this future. As you describe details of your future vision, there will be feelings associated with that experience.

Excitement, duty, liberation, joy, generosity, vindication, happiness and perhaps other words will express feelings that come from a powerful vision of the future.

Phrases like "find your passion," "live your purpose," and others are used to encourage people to look deep into themselves and find that place that connects with who they really are.

Often, we think "I'll be happy when I get (fill in the blank) ______________________________." Frequently, the words in the blank are fake, borrowed from someone else's vision, or a rejection of the struggles of the present. "I'll be happy when..." is not a motivating starting point.

Taking time to explore the feelings associated with the result you want will add power and motivation to creating the future you describe.

Sometimes such a vision may be connected to a "life purpose," but that's not a requirement. You may have a grand desire to serve others, perform a specific service, or further a worthy cause, like literacy, clean water, or another global challenge.

Alternatively, you may have a real desire to create something more near term that is powerful and valuable but not identified with a "life purpose."

Whether you've connected your result to a grand vision or a practical need you've failed to achieve so far, connecting the deep feelings you have now with those you anticipate when you cross the finish line is a crucial piece of creating the power to get it done.

After you have clearly stated your inspiring vision, the next assignment is to express the feelings you have about this future state. For each detail you described above, write down a *feeling* that you expect will accompany that detail.

For example, if your achievement is having a large house overlooking the ocean, and one of the details was a panoramic window facing the beach, then the description of the feeling would answer the question "What goes through your heart and your body as you stand in the house gazing at the ocean through that window?"

Write the detail, and then describe the accompanying feeling below:

Vision Detail #1:

____

____

____

____

____

____

Feeling You Experience:

____

____

____

____

____

____

Vision Detail #2:

____

____

____

____

____

____

Feeling You Experience:

____

____

____

____

____

____

Vision Detail #3:

Feeling You Experience:

Vision Detail #4:

Feeling You Experience:

Vision Detail #5:

Feeling You Experience:

Vision Detail #6:

Feeling You Experience:

Vision Detail #7:

Feeling You Experience:

____

____

____

____

____

____

Use as much paper as you need to make this thorough and complete. Avoid doing this only in your mind or on a computer. Writing is visceral and essential. This will make sure you don't shortchange this part of the exercise. The greater the depth of feeling, the greater the motivation.

Declare a Total Commitment

This is the last part of "Creating the Future." It's easy to say and hard to do.

Achieving a result that is significantly different from your status quo means you must *change* what you're doing *now*. You cannot obtain a new result through the same actions you take today.

You know that intuitively, but it's often hard to accept. We pretend there is some other way. We want the results without the work.

The world is full of people who daydream and imagine awesome achievements that never materialize. Perhaps you have been one of them. The truth is that things will stay the same until you choose to create the total commitment required to get to that new place of your vision.

When we think about total commitment, we must dig deep in our hearts for the reasons behind the vision. We've already explored the feelings in detail, but *reasons* are the bedrock of achievement.

Why do you want that vision? Do you know? Is it:

- Because you're supposed to?
- To be rich?
- To be famous?
- To be important?
- To prove to someone that you're good enough?

I have created achievements for all these reasons, and maybe you have too — none of them last very long.

If your goal is essential and you dig truthfully inside, you'll find reasons that rest on the bedrock of your soul. When your reasons come from the core of your being, then it's certain that your vision will come to fruition.

There will not be a one-to-one correlation between the details you list, the feelings you anticipate and the reasons you express for this achievement. There *will* be, at the most basic level, two or three powerful drivers that motivate you with unending power.

When you access that level of reason which often sounds like, "It's just who I am," or "It's just what I want," then you're coming to the bedrock which needs no further explanation.

Remember what I said at the start of this chapter. Creating the future is the process of building the image of a future state in such a powerful way that it perpetually fires the drive to make it real.

If you're looking at a difficult challenge or a result that has consistently eluded you, then you need concrete and specific answers to the following questions:

1. What would I be willing to *do* to have this?
2. What would I be willing to *start* doing?
3. What would I be willing to *stop* doing?
4. What *habits* would I be willing to change?
5. Which *beliefs* am I willing to give up or alter?
6. Am I willing to *die* for this?
7. Am I willing to *live* for this?

Not all results require life-and-death decisions. Most do not. However, changing long-standing habits or beliefs often feels like a life-and-death choice.

Think for a minute about someone who has continually been overweight, has severe health problems and still can't give up junk food, or someone who has cancer and won't quit smoking. We often feel completely bound by past practice and powerless to move forward.

Clearly articulating what you're willing to do, or not do, to achieve this result is the only secure foundation of a "total commitment."

What changes in my life am I willing to make to achieve the result?

Examples might be:

- Habits I'm willing to give up.
- Hobbies I'm willing to postpone.
- Time wasters I'm willing to stop.
- New habits I'm willing to form.
- Fears I'm willing to overcome.
- Hard choices I'm willing to make.
- Others as needed.

In the space below write down your specific commitments.

____

____

____

____

____

____

____

____

It doesn't have to be perfect. You can adjust it as needed. The very nature of accomplishing difficult things requires iteration. Just get started and add items as needed.

If you feel discouraged at any point, revisit the Mental Earthquake step. Don't stay discouraged. Exercise your creativity. Invest in yourself by hiring a coach. Love yourself more deeply and show it.

Chapter 29

CP = Courageous Planning

"There is one thing that is true about planning... whatever you plan, it will be wrong!"

The purpose of CP is to learn effective planning and to make your plan a trusted friend.

The first rule of planning: Whatever you plan, it will be wrong. So, If we know a plan will be wrong, why bother planning at all and how does a plan become a trusted friend?

That is a good question. I'm not saying that planning is unnecessary, or doesn't deserve focus and attention. I am saying the best plans cannot wholly and accurately anticipate future conditions, and consequently, will never be executed as created.

Combining uncertainty about planning with a natural tendency to skip over hard things leads to a sad truth. Most plans are poorly conceived, hastily created and therefore generally ineffective.

We could say, "Let's get started, move forward and figure it out as we go." That approach might work for a few things. Sometimes, passion for the project and excitement of the unknown leads to completion. More often, it leads to frustration, delays, discouragement, and ultimately, abandonment.

So...what does it take to make a good plan? What are the characteristics of effective planning? Many courses and even degrees are available to teach planning. Each approach has strengths and drawbacks. I'm not endorsing a particular project planning and management scheme. Instead, the results equation gives you a framework that will mesh with any good planning approach.

Sometimes we confuse planning with goal setting. Setting the goals is just one part. For example, One goal setting mechanism uses the acronym SMART.

Goals must be Specific, Measurable, Achievable, Realistic and Time-bound.

As an acronym, that's a nice way to think about the characteristics of goals, but it's inadequate for proper planning, particularly with challenging projects full of complexity, long duration, high difficulty, many external barriers or interior roadblocks.

A Courageous Plan starts with two simple questions

Do What? By When?

In its simplest form, a plan is a statement of completion that answers two questions. Do What? By When? The description of "Do what?" must match the result specified at the beginning, and contain the details generated in "Creating the Future."

The level of detail depends on the achievement. There must be enough detail to create clarity about the outcome. This could include functional and performance specifications, customer expectations, and other metrics as required.

"By when?" also comes from the result statement created at the beginning of the equation. It's critical that you are clear about the precise nature of the result, and the specific target date.

Effective plans have common characteristics besides clear results and end dates. The first of these are milestones. This is particularly important for projects that take more time, have a broad scope, or involve many teams or parts. Milestones measure progress and let us know if we are on track to meet overall objectives.

Accompanying the milestones, which specify measurable progress along the path, we have timelines, which are expected completion dates of the milestones.

Milestones and Timelines show progress and tell whether the project will be completed on time. In addition to tracking timelines, expenditure milestones may be appropriate depending on the project. This allows the project manager to track the completion stage, timelines and budget.

The third element in successful plans are incentives. With complex projects, it's common practice to have compensation, recognition, or future considerations tied to achievement of milestones, on-time and on budget. These incentives can create motivation and maintain momentum for execution.

This same concept, applied to personal objectives or plans created by a solopreneur or small business, will have the same effect. Looking forward to some incentive can be a significant driver to keep people on track and motivated.

This simple trilogy, "timelines, milestones, and incentives," is obvious when described in this fashion. I'm continually surprised at how many entrepreneurs and small companies move forward with vaguely formed ideas, ignoring the milestones, hoping things work out and the attitude of "just grind it out until it's done."

Not surprisingly, this brings with it a poor completion rate and discouragement that sidelines so many entrepreneurial dreams.

The heart of the Courageous Plan is the Step Map. The concept is simple, but lack of detail and organization provided by a step map, particularly in the case of small business or solopreneur, is a major cause of failure.

Create Your Results Equation™ Step Map:

Step 1 – Create the Master Brain Dump

List every element, action, or process that must be completed to achieve your result. Depending on the project, this may include one or more people. This is a brain dump and not in any particular order.

For example, one objective frequently sought by entrepreneurs is, "Create a product I can sell online." If that's what you want, then steps would include at least the following:

a. Identify the target audience you serve.
b. What does your client want or need?
c. What level of knowledge are your clients at?
d. What will the learning curve entail?
e. What will they know, experience, or be able to *do* or *feel* at the end?
f. Who else is trying to meet this need?
g. What do competitors sell?
h. Why are you better?
i. What is your unique addition to the existing library of the solution?
j. What type of content will you create? (videos, PDFs, assessment tools, seminars, and so on.)
k. Choose the delivery system (membership site, home study, group coaching, or other.)

l. Set the likely price point.
m. Spell out the follow-up product or strategy.
n. Etc.

The is not a complete list of actions to create a product or service. It's a partial list to illustrate Step 1. There would be many other elements.

For example, the list doesn't include an analysis to decide how this product fits into your company's overall product offerings or the creation of marketing campaigns or sales channels.

Those considerations and others must be done before you decide to create the product or concurrently with production.

Performing a brain dump of everything required for the goal is the starting point to create a Step Map.

It's necessary to go over the list several times to get everything on paper, and even then, you'll likely add things to the list as you move further into the process.

A common question is: "How detailed does the list need to be?" The answer depends on your experience with this type of achievement, your history of success on completing projects and your knowledge of the Results Equation™.

To illustrate, let's break down step j) from the list above, which is the type of content to create. Unless you're experienced in creating courses and the associated processes, this step will contain several sub-parts. For example, you will need to know the preferred content medium of your audience, your skill at writing, editing or video production and the budget you might need.

There are three keys to making this work:

- Please don't get bogged down in extraordinary detail so that it's cumbersome and a waste of time.
- Don't be so high-level so that you leave out intricate details that could derail your timeline.
- Do create enough detail, so it feels manageable and allows for everyone required to be involved.

Only your previous experience with similar projects and your experience with the equation will help you gauge an appropriate level of detail.

Shortcuts to get this done more effectively will come from experience with success and failure, research, talking to people who have done similar projects, courses that you might take, and most of all, a coach who can guide your efforts and keep you from getting bogged down.

Depending on the project, the list might be fifty, one hundred, or more items. It may make sense to break the project down into smaller chunks. Again, help from people who've done this before is your biggest asset.

Step 2 – Create the Sequence

Take the brain dump from Step one and put them in a logical sequence. This sequencing may require a critical path analysis to make sure you don't create unexpected bottlenecks or delays.

This is a little bit like planning a college degree. Some coursework is done in a particular order. You can do some things in parallel. If you screw it up, you'll take six years to get a four-year degree.

Now that the steps are in order list them in the left column of a spreadsheet either on a computer or paper. I use large art paper and colored markers because I enjoy writing by hand.

Step 3 – Assign Tasks

In the second column write down *who* is responsible for completing this item from the first column. If you're doing everything yourself and your name will be after every item, then omit this column.

If you have a team, the names of the relevant team member go there. If you are outsourcing part of it, then note that.

If you don't know who will complete certain items, then instead of a name, put a date by which you'll assign the task. Completing those assignment decisions may be another step. Be sure you remember the overall project timelines.

Step 4 – Develop Budgets

The third column is an estimate of the cost associated with each step. If you're doing the creation yourself, this estimate is zero. If you need to buy a tool or a video background or hire someone, then there is an expense associated with that step. You may need a step to find contractors.

Managing those expenses is a budgeting process that your business needs to do. Depending on the size of the costs, and the budget impacts, you may need a Step Map to create the cash necessary for the investment.

Step 5 – Estimate Time

In the last column estimate how long it'll take you to complete that step. This number should always be in hours. If you find that your estimate is in days or weeks, then that step is too big and needs to be broken down into smaller chunks.

If you're outsourcing part of the project, then this is the contractual completion date for your contractor. Don't forget to include steps for your time in managing or interfacing with them. This is not a trivial time requirement.

For example, if you've contracted video editing in your course creation, then you need appropriate steps on the map to keep track of completion milestones, approval check-ins and other processes necessary to make sure you and your contractor hit a home run and not a series of foul balls.

Don't stumble with perfection. The project is the goal, not the spreadsheet. As you create the Step Map and during the project, you will create several revisions. This is expected.

How you do the step map will depend on your personal style. Some love the convenience of a computer spreadsheet because it is easier to move things around. For me, that's too impersonal.

I use big sheets of art paper and different colored markers. It takes longer, but the process of writing and re-writing lets me process ideas and increases my creativity. This is especially true when there are several parallel processes.

I use a different color for each step that can be done independently of other steps. That way I can see the critical path in all areas at the same time.

You will develop your own flow in creating these. Don't get so enamored with the artwork that it wastes time. This is a functional tool that is only as good as you make it. Use the Step Map to ensure nothing is missed; to create critical paths, to avoid delays, develop budgets and help you set realistic completion deadlines.

When you've finished your Step Map, you should be able to look at it and feel satisfied and confident. You should be able to say with certainty, "If I do all of these things, in this order, then I know for *sure* this project will get done."

If looking at the map doesn't produce this feeling, then go through it again to see if you believe your time estimates are accurate. Perhaps you've left out steps, forgot hidden costs or glossed over something important that somehow shortchanges the process.

The Overlay

Now that the Step Map is created, this is where the rubber meets the road. Often, when we are making a significant change, it is *on top* of everything else we're doing. You have a life to live and other obligations besides completing the Step Map tasks assigned to you and managing steps assigned to others.

"Doing this part well means life or death for your project. It's simple but overlooked, and consequently creates a point of procrastination, struggle, frustration and ultimately failure."

Now that you have a total estimate of the hours required to finish the project, you have to see where they fit in your life. Get out your calendar and block off the hours that you've estimated to complete your project. Start with the first steps and move through the Step Map until you've covered everything.

Block in time for supervisory activities if you have contractors or team members. Use your experience to gauge the accuracy of your estimates. If you don't know, do a bit of research or talk with others to get a good idea.

Then, add a contingency buffer to each time estimate. Nothing ever goes as planned. If you don't add a buffer, the minute something goes off track it can feel like the end of the world. To start with, I find it useful to add a 30% buffer to every time estimate.

For example, when I'm creating a video, and I estimate that it'll take 10 hours to shoot and edit one part of the project, I always budget 13 hours. Experience has taught me that I need a 30% cushion, or I will always be late. The part that takes longer varies from project to project, but there is always something.

What your "safety margin" should be will depend on your track record with estimation. The key here is to acknowledge that you don't have infinite time for the project, you have other things to do, and it must all fit into your life.

If you have soccer games to attend, a spouse that needs attention, church or community activities that you support or other obligations that are part of your life, then those must all be accommodated in the schedule, or you'll end up being frustrated.

This is so important that I must repeat it. Failure to schedule the hours indicated by the Step Map is the first guarantee of failure. Failure to add a safety margin is the second. Failure to add supervisory time if you've outsourced parts is the third.

This is not rocket science, but I am continually amazed at the inability or unwillingness of people to put it down on paper and then into their schedules. Perhaps we don't want to face the reality of the schedule. Perhaps we want to live in la-la land and "hope it will happen." Either way, the schedule is the key and omitting this part is a recipe for quitting the project.

Adjustments

No plan goes as initially designed. Things break, money is not available on time, stuff takes much longer than planned and more. Periodic review and adjustment must be built into any plan that takes more than a few days to complete.

Once a week, you need to do three things:

- Review the Step Map and check off items that are completed.
- Celebrate and reward yourself with the incentives you planned at given milestones. Keep a positive atmosphere around the work.

- Manage unexpected delays. If things haven't worked out as planned, then make the necessary adjustments in the Step Map, and reflect those adjustments in your calendar.

When you start making adjustments, you come face to face with another reality of project management: the final due date. If you discover early on that modifications will delay the final due date, identify that as early as possible, so you have time to make decisions about how to manage this.

If the end date is flexible, then move the schedule blocks and start again. If you are up against an external deadline and can't extend it, then you must find the hours.

You don't find missing hours with wishful thinking. You find them by making explicit trades in your schedule. That means you delete other activities you planned and put in the appropriate work blocks. Failure to block hours in the schedule and make explicit trades by eliminating other activities creates stress, reduced capacity, strains in affected relationships and is a key ingredient to failure.

You alone will know what you can trade. Perhaps you have unscheduled time. Maybe there are social activities, television time and other innocent but time-consuming pastimes that you can omit.

If you can't find the time, then you need to change the deadline or get some help. Whatever you do, don't ignore the problem, because it does not go away, and the stress created by leaving it unsolved damages creativity and efficiency.

Handling the situation and managing your apportionment of time across your whole life reduces stress, and gives you confidence in your ability to complete the project on schedule and budget.

Work-Backs

Another effective use of the Step Map is for projects with a fixed deadline. After the Step Map is created and you lay out the requirements, you put the time in your calendar working back from the deadline. That way you can see if there are enough hours between today and the due date.

If the start date should have been two weeks ago, then you have three choices.

1. Renegotiate the project timelines.
2. Modify your existing schedule to create the time you need to finish the project.
3. Get more help so that the project fits without you becoming sleep deprived.

Pretending the time will somehow magically appear or believing that you can do things "faster" is a poor strategy, and will create stress, mistakes, and ultimately, a missed deadline.

Minimum Daily Accomplishments

Regardless of how effectively we plan, or how diligently we schedule, some days don't work out the way we intended. Interruptions occur. Incidental mayhem ensues without warning, or other things get in the way – a flat tire, a sick child, etc.

When this happens, we often feel like giving up, wasting the rest of the day and vowing to start again tomorrow. It's normal to feel frustrated and discouraged when things derail our plans. When it all falls apart, you can go back to the "Mental Earthquake" section to make your power "rumble on command."

One way to make that happen is to create a "minimum daily accomplishment." Think about a strenuous hike. When you feel tired, and want to quit, you look ahead and say, "If I can just get to that peak up there, then I can rest and maybe stop for the night." This is a version of the "milestones" in "Creating the Future," that helps you keep moving today.

One way to do this is with your morning planning. When you start the day, you know what you expect to complete. At the same time, you can pick something that, no matter what, you will get finished that day. It needs to be reasonable and doable.

If the day goes well and you blow past your minimum goal, pat yourself on the back and feel good for a job well done, and a day well spent.

If disaster strikes and you feel like giving up, having just "one thing" that you will complete that day is a powerful tool. It allows you to end the day with a feeling of accomplishment, instead of disappointment, discouragement, or shame.

Minimum Viable Product

Another tip for planning, particularly for entrepreneurs and online business people, is the "Minimum Viable Product." Often, in the initial stages of planning, we have grandiose dreams about what we will get done in an optimistic timeframe.

It is common to realize at some point that we bit off far more than we could chew. For example, the course you are creating may turn out to require more work than you realized.

This is where the concept of "Minimum Viable Product" comes in handy. When we realize we have a tiger by the tail, we want to give up and bury our head in the sand. This translates quickly into not getting anything done.

Another way to think about this is to shrink the scope of the product. What would be the *minimum* product that your customers would love? Is there something that serves them and solves a real problem, but is easier to create than the original product you imagined?

This means quickly adjusting some portions of the Step Map and adjusting timing schedules. This is far preferable to simply giving up and declaring it "too hard to do."

The concept of minimum viable product has rescued many ideas from the product graveyard and their creators from the frustration of failure.

Take time *now* and work through the first iteration of your project Step Map on the computer or a large sheet of paper. Do it carefully and estimate as necessary. Just get it done.

Be patient with yourself and iterate two or three times. Refer to these instructions and get other help you might need to accomplish this indispensable piece of the equation. Remember – the Results Equation™ is not a linear process.

In the next module, "Relentless Execution," we discuss the need to "Execute, Evaluate, Adjust." As you do the step map, don't get stuck in the evaluation part of the process. Keep moving. Also, don't assume that moving once through the process will create magic and remove all obstacles.

Go after it and have fun. The nature of accomplishing difficult things requires iteration and practice. Don't be discouraged. Don't quit. Exercise patience and creativity. Hire a coach. Celebrate your gifts and talents by remembering that you will get to the goal line if you keep moving.

Chapter 30

RE = Relentless Execution

"Nothing happens without execution!"

It is easy to say, "Just Do It," or to tell someone to "suck it up and keep going." Relentless Execution (RE) is not about yelling at yourself or others and hoping this will keep us moving through obstacles.

We don't work like that. We react to our circumstances and emotional stories. We live in the context of our beliefs, constraints and what we do day to day.

We know we work better when we feel good, and when we believe we are doing good. We stay engaged if we believe in our project. We have good days and bad days.

The foundational principle in this module is that you have control over your own experience. The purpose of RE is to learn to take responsibility and control of every day. You control your experiences, your happiness, and productivity each day. Do not give it away.

Regardless of mental earthquakes, amazing visions, and awesome planning, nothing happens without execution. This is obvious but does not leverage the power of that truth.

You could say, "Obviously, you just go *do* stuff, so why an entire section on getting stuff done?" Well, if it were that simple, everyone would be successful and wealthy, and you wouldn't be reading this book. It's not simple. The process of execution and particularly *relentless* execution is as elusive as the Abominable Snowman.

Like everything else, there is art and science to execution. This section will teach that art and science. It follows the other steps because activity without focus and direction is like the proverbial chicken with no head.

So, what's the difference between frantic activity and relentless execution?

I define "execution" as "specific action steps intentionally driven toward a particular outcome." Relentless means "without stopping, despite opposition, in spite of hindrances or without distraction."

Putting it all together, "Relentless Execution" means "the continuous and repeated process of taking specific action steps intentionally driven toward a particular outcome without stopping and despite opposition."

Any goal worth achieving will have setbacks, struggles, and periods of confusion. Returning to the example of getting in physical shape, it's easy to see that after beginning a workout regime, sore muscles, slow progress, lack of motivation, and other obstacles can get in the way.

With a focus on the goal, a clear internal vision of the feelings and benefits of being in shape, a clear and absolute commitment to move through any obstacles and a robust accountability system, relentless execution will bring the desired result.

Dealing with Reality

Every day is not created equal. Our bodies feel different, our minds are in different places, and events around us impact what we think, how we feel and what we get done. Instead of living at the mercy of external events, what would happen to your focus and execution if every day was a great day?

What do you do to optimize performance, while at the same time, accepting what *is*, and loving every moment of life? That sounds like a tall order, so let's discuss some tools that make this happen.

To simplify, let's assume there are three kinds of days:

1. **Great days.** You start on time, you feel good, you keep on schedule, and things move along well. Like riding a bike with a tailwind.

2. **Mediocre days.** Something isn't perfect about the morning. You get up late, you have a disagreement at home, you get stuck in traffic, or the internet is down. Maybe you get interrupted a lot. A few people don't do what you need, or something doesn't work out. You push through the day and hope tomorrow is better.

3. **Horrible days.** Everything you do seems to go wrong. You don't feel so good. You may believe you're doing the wrong things, or you have no hope of success. You want to throw in the towel, veg out and vanish.

I regularly ask clients and prospects on how they rate their days. On average, people report about 80% of their days fall into category #2 – Mediocre days. 15% are in category #3 – Horrible days and 5% or less fall into category #1 – Great days. I was surprised at the relative consistency of the responses.

This is clearly subjective. Your perception may be completely different. If it is, that is great! The point is that most people believe their time and effort isn't optimized and many external things control the quality of their day.

Whatever your numbers are, imagine what would happen if you moved to 75% or more Great days.

There are two parts to making this shift happen.

- The first is creating a great day in the morning. This is done by intentionally having a morning ritual that connects you to your being and your purpose.

- The second is to have tools to reclaim the day when things go off the rails.

Morning Ritual

Creating a morning ritual is the most powerful tool I have ever used or taught to help you meet the day in your most potent resourceful state.

My morning ritual consists of the exercises in the Mental Earthquake module plus the acronym SPEM-B which stands for Spiritual, Physical, Emotional, Mental and Business.

I spend at least 10-15 minutes focusing on each area in the acronym to remind me who am and what I am about in the world. For example:

- **Spiritual** – Reading sacred literature, engaging in meditation and prayer.
- **Physical** – Stretching, yoga or Qi Gong.
- **Emotional** – Thinking about a relationship I want to nurture or repair and then sending a text or writing a note to someone to express that nurturing.
- **Mental** – Reading 1 or 2 chapters in a book I find stimulating and challenging.
- **Business** – If today is a work day, then this is done when I start work. If this is a non-work day, I reflect for a time on the state of things and what needs my attention.

I do this in solitude and quiet, so my mind is clear and at peace. This is not to say that there is no other part of the day devoted to these areas of life. Perhaps you are working out with a friend tonight, or you have a visit planned with someone.

This morning preparation is in addition to that time. This process is a survey and focuses through all through areas of life at the start of the day, so I can plan effectively and make sure I am balanced.

The ritual is changed regularly to include and focus on whatever creates the most power for me. The key is that I never omit this practice and I always complete it with intention and clarity.

Creating this habit takes practice but is well worth the effort. You can learn more about morning rituals and the power of meditation in the resources listed in the Appendix.

Reclaiming Difficult Days

The second part of becoming a powerhouse of relentless execution is learning to reclaim a day when you're interrupted continuously or where something's gone wrong.

First, remember that the quality of your day and your life is in your hands. You are the architect of your life. Second, have a set of tools you use to intentionally get you back on track and into the mode of growth and productivity.

Here are six tools that I use to accomplish the work of rescuing a day.

- 50/10 work chunks
- Meditation
- Re-connecting with my Vision
- Power Words
- Distraction to Focus
- The Person Across the Gap

50/10 Work Chunks

You can only work effectively for so long at a stretch. Numerous studies show that taking regular breaks increases effectiveness and productivity. It also has a positive effect on your body and your mood. Here is one powerful way to implement this principle.

Get two timers; you can buy inexpensive ones for a few dollars. Set one-timer for 50 minutes, and the other for 10 minutes.

Ideally, each timer should be a different color, lessening the chance of getting confused and re-setting the wrong one. This makes everything much easier.

Begin your work chunk by starting your 50-minute countdown timer. Your commitment during this work time is a total focus on the project at hand: no distractions, no email, no messages, no interruptions.

Do not answer the phone, do *nothing* except work on the project. Fifty minutes isn't too long to focus. Having *zero interruptions* is critical.

Because you have a timer set, you know you won't miss any appointments, the world won't fall apart, and nothing is going to explode as you work on your project for 50 minutes.

The timer is liberating. You have nothing else to worry about except whatever you've committed to doing for that 50-minute block. Face the timer away from you so you can't even check how long is left.

Doing this allows you to focus, knowing perfectly well that the timer will beep when the time is up. When the timer beeps, get to a convenient stopping point and stop.

Now, grab the 10-minute timer. Stand up, move away from your workspace and do something else for 10 minutes.

Take a walk, stretch, or do something else that is relaxing for your body and mind. Make this is a time to review your declarations or celebrate what you've done.

Enjoy the feeling of having successfully completed the block and treat yourself to some self-love and appreciation.

You will develop your own form of relaxation, and after you experiment with several different activities, you'll find those that are most effective and rewarding.

After the 10-minute timer goes off, wind down the relaxation and move back into the next 50-minute block, repeat this process no more than three times before taking a more extended break, perhaps eating something or otherwise nourishing your body and spirit.

Fifty minutes isn't the magic block of work time. Experiment with what works best for you. If your habits have been so scattered that you find it difficult to focus for 50 minutes, start with a shorter interval, and gradually increase it until you find yourself feeling most effective.

One client thought it necessary to begin with 15/5 minute time blocks. Whatever creates the ability for you to free yourself from distraction is the right answer for you.

Meditation

Meditation is a word that's often misunderstood. Sometimes it's associated with religious disciplines and practices. I'm using it here in a more straightforward way.

For our purposes, meditation is the intentional practice of taking a few minutes to relax the body, mind, and spirit. The skill of learning to relax and focus is valuable beyond my ability to articulate.

While seemingly simple, our usual practice is to allow random thoughts and external input to govern most of our waking hours. We don't develop our ability to focus our thoughts and direct them where we want them to go.

Learning to meditate by focusing on the breath or in some other way, allows you to develop the skill of directing your thinking.

While it is beyond the scope of this book to teach meditation, there are resources in the Appendix if you want additional instruction.

The critical thing here is not to over-complicate the process, just set aside time and begin learning how to relax your body, mind, and spirit.

It's often suggested to focus on breathing. There are several reasons for this, and I'll give you just a couple. First, your breath is natural, repetitive, and always with you. Second, you need no special equipment or circumstances. You can do it in the middle of a crowd or a noisy room.

Focus your mind on the experience of breathing in and breathing out, with all its nuances and detail. When intruding thoughts draw your mind away from the breath, as they undoubtedly will, acknowledge their existence, and intentionally bring your mind back to the breath.

This simple process begins to develop the skill of directing your mind. As this skill improves, you will be able to direct your mind away from distracting or negative thinking. You will be able to direct it toward positive and energizing ideas and thus control the feelings in your body.

Allowing yourself to focus purely on the present is powerful. A lot has been written on being in the "now." You can't change the past, and your only hope of affecting the future lies in the present.

We spend an enormous amount of time fretting about or regretting something we can't change. We spend a similar amount of time dreading, hoping or fussing about the future. Staying in the present helps you create the kind of results that others envy, in record time and with great pleasure.

For example, one effect of meditation is to slow the brain waves from the normal Beta state to the lower Alpha range. In the alpha range, we are more productive, more focused and more creative.

This is described as "being in flow." Meditation will teach you what it feels like to be in flow and more importantly, teach you the skill to get into flow any time you wish.

This will dramatically increase your execution results, eliminate stress, and create joy as you build the results you desire.

Re-Connect with Your Vision

Another tool when you are distracted or discouraged is to go back and revisit the future vision you created in the "Create the Future" (CF) section.

Reconnecting with the details, feelings, and reasons thoughtfully and compellingly can restore motivation and minimize discouragement and fatigue.

Combining this with meditation is a powerful way to augment the force exerted by your vision, and exponentially restore power to your efforts. This is particularly important when you've been discouraged, had setbacks, or had things not work out as intended.

Creating a powerful vision in the CF section is critical for this to work. If you skimped when you created the future, it would have less power for you now. If you find your vision isn't compelling, return to that section and beef it up until it energizes you beyond measure every time you think about it.

Power Words

We know words matter. Often, we think that they don't matter *much*. Nothing could be further from the truth. Your internal dialogue, as well as your external statements, shape your expectation of the future.

Creating "Power Words" that describe the essence of your core beliefs will keep you grounded and restore energy and faith in the result you want.

I am not talking about a set of "wishes" you repeat over and over like a poem or mantra. I'm talking about words which energize your soul and connect with your real sense of being and purpose as a divine creator.

It's not essential that they be perfect. It's not important that they're the be-all and end-all of everything you ever say. What *is* important is that when you say these words out loud, they create a connection and a sense of purpose about your life and goals.

For example, my words are: "Love, Create, Serve." It took me many years to come to a final set of words that capture the essence of who I am and what I'm about.

LOVE is first because it's the foundation of success. Any success not based on genuine concern and caring for blessing the lives of others is short-lived and empty. Many who have achieved high levels of success or made lots of money, find it empty and continually search for another source of fulfillment.

Perhaps this is something you've experienced yourself, such as setting a major goal, achieving it and then finding it didn't carry the impact in your heart you wanted. For me, starting from a place of love is the foundation that gives meaning to everything else I do.

CREATE is an expression of our ability and obligation as divine entities to express our unique gifts and talents and create things of value and usefulness. Developing and expressing your gifts is the fastest way to become skilled and valuable and make your biggest contribution.

SERVE is an expression of the attitude I take towards life in general. Everything for me is about how I can serve those around me. My journey has taught me that my own needs are abundantly met and with plenty to spare when I am busy serving others.

My power words are something I refer to regularly as I plan my day and execute my strategies – particularly when things go wrong, and there is a struggle. Referring to these words creates a place of comfort and energy.

Creating your own power words, even if they change over time, gives you an anchor and a reference point to revitalize your execution when your focus is lagging.

Distraction to Focus

Another valuable tool is to have a strategy that moves you out of distraction. One of the most potent attention getters is vigorous movement.

If you find yourself surfing the Internet, falling asleep, bored, tired, or otherwise fully-distracted from what you had planned, jump up from your chair and get outside. This is particularly effective if it's cold. Walk or even run down the block.

If going outside isn't an option, then stand away from your workspace and do some squats or run in place. Doing something that requires vigorous physical activity will pull your mind from distraction.

If you're engaging in negative self-talk or discouraging thinking, this exercise will be especially effective for you. Hitting the floor to do 20 push-ups will focus your mind. When you're doing push-ups, you can't do or think about anything else except push-ups.

After you've done enough push-ups or running in place to be tired, you kill the mental distraction. Breathe deeply, get some water and then choose how you wish to focus.

A key to making this work is the action you choose must be all-consuming.

Going for a leisurely walk does not change your mental focus. It's easy to continue the distracting train of thought if you do something that doesn't command attention. Jumping jacks, squats, burpees, push-ups all fit the bill.

Vigorous exercise is immediately available and effective, and therefore something you can do almost anywhere and anytime. If exertion is not feasible, then active stretching can substitute, like bending over to touch your toes several times.

The Person Across the Gap

We all know what it feels like when we achieve goals. We completed the task. We climbed the mountain. We can see ourselves in that future state. I call that "The Person Across the Gap."

That successful person embodies everything you wish to become. It is you *after* you achieve your goal. It is the future you, in great shape, having the connections, relationships, cash, and self-confidence you're committed to creating.

When you find yourself discouraged, stuck, or uncertain about what to do, take a moment and reflect. Ask yourself, "What would the person across the gap do in this situation?"

You'll find it easy to answer that question in almost every situation. You know, almost without hesitation, what represents the *best* action in your current circumstances. Often, we lack the courage or determination to do *that* thing, but we always *know* what it is.

Ask yourself this question out loud and say the answer out loud. Then just declare "Okay, if that's what my future-self, across the gap, would do, then that's what I choose to do *now*."

Making this declaration out loud increases the power and the likelihood that you'll do what you said. There is something about audible repetition that increases the likelihood of compliance.

Regularly and actively using these tools and others that you devise for your circumstance, will completely change your daily experience. You'll soon find yourself taking control of your time and projects and executing more effectively. You will have great days.

The last two parts in Relentless Execution are habits that increase your effectiveness and the likelihood of success. You can develop these habits if you don't have them now.

Ready, Fire, Steer or "RFS"

The traditional saying is, "ready, aim, fire." That sequence expresses preparation and then action. It also allows for procrastination. Then it becomes "ready, aim, aim, aim, aim…". Sometimes this is called "paralysis by analysis." It's rooted in fear and usually gets in the way.

Things change rapidly enough that we often need to take action and *then* make adjustments on the way. Action reveals the truth of our preparation.

That distinction is represented by the principle, "ready, fire, steer." Action is the fastest way to decide if what you're doing is moving you closer or further away from your goal. Action creates clarity about both purpose and tactics.

Practical examples of this include split-testing headlines for email copy or split-testing videos to see which is most effective, or experimenting with different product features to discover customer response rates.

Waiting until you're fully prepared is a recipe for stagnation. There will never be a perfect time to take the next action. NOW is the time for action; action will immediately reveal its effectiveness and allow you to make adjustments. This constitutes the "steering" described in this approach.

You must overcome your fear of being wrong. One way to describe this is to "*fail forward fast*." Rarely are results exactly as planned. Expect to fail to some degree every time you act.

The fear that missing the mark is somehow a reflection on you or your idea is merely a distraction and lowers confidence and self-esteem. Approach every day with the question, "What can I do *now* that moves me toward my goal?"

E^2A or Execute, Evaluate, Adjust

The second principle goes hand in hand with the first. "Ready, Fire, Steer," is the approach to relentless execution. "Execute, Evaluate, Adjust," creates regular process improvements and grows success.

As part of your "Courageous Plan," setting a regular schedule for evaluation of milestones and timelines is a critical part of keeping your execution on track.

Having an intentional and regularly-scheduled evaluation allows you to regroup and gather focus, especially when things go south or stagnate.

Evaluation consists of two parts. First is your assessment of the success of a given step in the Step Map. Second, gathering feedback from team members or customers is critical in measuring the effectiveness of a given step.

In this framework, it's essential to view these evaluations as *data points* designed to improve your product and speed of execution. These are not tribunals about your character.

If you maintain the focus that your goal is to *serve* those you *can,* with the *best* product in the *best fashion* available to you, then the idea of diminished self-esteem or confidence from a temporary failure falls off the table.

Exercises:

In the space below, or on a separate piece of paper, describe the morning ritual you'll use to create the best version of yourself to begin each day: Remember this will change as you experiment and decide what works best.

Describe how you'll use the tools to recapture bad days and change your outlook when trouble strikes. This will change as you experiment to find those most effective for you. Be specific about what you commit to doing so that these actions will have the greatest impact:

____

____

____

____

____

____

____

____

____

____

Describe how you'll apply the attitude of, "Ready, Fire, Steer" as you approach each execution step in your "Courageous Plan."

Describe how you'll use the principle of "Execute, Evaluate, Adjust." Make sure your reviews are regular and keep your "Courageous Plan" current and effective. How often will you take the time to review your progress and make adjustments?

Remember…the results equation isn't a linear process.

Remember, don't get stuck in judgment when you "Execute, Evaluate, Adjust." Don't engage in the drama of failure and the need to adjust plans and actions as you go along.

Don't assume that completing each step once will create magic and remove all obstacles.

The nature of difficult achievement requires iteration and practice. Iteration and practice are the heart and soul of achievement.

Become a Relentless Execution Warrior. Don't buy into failure. Keep moving on the path. Exercise your creativity and invest in yourself by hiring a coach. Express your gifts and celebrate your successes in a way that shares your light and makes your life fabulous.

Chapter 31

Putting It All Together

Thousands have books have been written about the individual parts contained in The Results Equation. The advice and processes in those books are generally good and powerful.

As I have studied and used countless resources over the years, what I find missing is a comprehensive treatment of the process required to create a result. Specifically a process that deals with both the tangible and intangible parts of the journey.

A fabulous book on planning or an excellent system for tracking progress is only a small part of what happens when someone decides to make a change and create an outcome.

This is especially true when you own a small business, work for yourself, or you are working on a personal project.

In a corporate setting, simplifying assumptions mask much of the work required to stay motivated and keep moving. Corporations just assume people show up and are productive.

As you saw in the section on "Courageous Planning," the overlay matching the projected time requirements to your available calendar time is key. This calculation is assumed away in most corporate planning processes.

The focus on the "truth" in the equation is also unique among literature about achievement. Whole systems about getting things done have been created with a simplifying assumption that you are able and willing to operate from a place of truth.

We know this isn't true. We know that we constantly lie to ourselves. We know we make promises we don't keep, and this creates an atmosphere of "maybe" around every commitment.

You see this in the language we have in our conversation. If we tell someone we will do something; we say "I'll be there," or "I will get that done."

Often, what we mean is:

- if I remember
- if I still feel like it
- if nothing better comes along
- if you don't make me mad between now and then.

If we want someone to understand we are committed, then we add all kinds of language like "no, I really mean it." "I swear, I really will do this or that."

You've heard this, and you've said it, so you know exactly what I mean. Right this minute you can think of someone whose word means exactly nothing. You have no idea if they will do what they commit to doing. The more casual the relationship, the more this is true.

Unfortunately, this is demonstrated most by our failure to keep commitments to ourselves. I've created the equation process on the premise that the way you do one thing, is the way you do everything.

Fundamentally this means that you must be true to yourself before you can be true or committed to anyone or anything else.

If you can't keep commitments to yourself, you won't keep commitments in other circumstances, or if you do, it'll be half-hearted and half-baked.

The equation is a comprehensive and deep system to help you to accomplish anything you desire in any setting required.

For example, the equation has demonstrated success in applications including the following:

- Health and fitness (100 pounds lost.)
- Business startup (successful product launch in under 90 days.)
- Book publishing (number one bestsellers.)
- Income growth (40 x income growth in one year.)
- Personal challenges (ending heroin addiction.)
- Fear of public speaking (Ted talk contender.)
- Successful management of complex stakeholder processes.
- Corporate reorganization.
- Corporate change management in a high-stress environment.
- Learning new skills and mastering complex processes.

- Eliminating fear.
- Ending procrastination.
- Obliterating self-sabotage.

...the list is endless.

Whatever the challenge might be, if you make the choices required, adopt the characteristics specified and follow the Results Equation, you can create any outcome you choose.

Part III

The Results Equation™ In the Real World

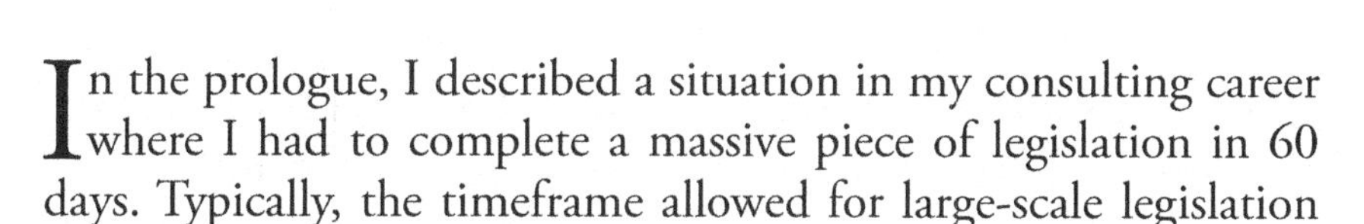

In the prologue, I described a situation in my consulting career where I had to complete a massive piece of legislation in 60 days. Typically, the timeframe allowed for large-scale legislation of this magnitude is two to three years.

The excitement of those present turned to fear and anger when I announced the timeframe. I wasn't worried, because I had a secret weapon – which had two parts.

First, I had done many "impossible" projects in my career and had become a specialist at creating results that seemed outside the bounds of possibility.

Second, I had The Results Equation. I hadn't formalized it into the process I have now, but I had used the principles repeatedly to create similar results.

Rather than argue or pump them up with rah-rah encouragement, I agreed without reservation that the task was impossible and that I would need to return to the Minister of Energy and tell him we were doomed to failure.

That ended all discussion about the scope and timing of the task because I agreed it couldn't be done. Remember that one key element for success is dropping the drama associated with challenging work.

I had long since learned that trying to convince people, who are in a heightened emotional state, was a lost cause. Instead, I began at the beginning.

Where are we now? What is the existing law? What are the reasons for creating the new Commission we were assigned to create? What would such a thing look like, regardless of the timeframe?

Going through the process of articulating the present reality and then creating a vibrant view of the future state, with the new Commission and its functions and processes in place, allowed everyone to focus on their area of expertise.

The meeting was long. It went smoothly, and we made great progress. Suddenly we had a vision of the future that was compelling and interesting.

The path to get there was quite thorny. Tens of billions of dollars were at stake. We talked about the process of stakeholder consultations. How many consultations would we conduct? What stakeholder groups would be involved? And, all the rest.

It's rare to open such a complex and significant legislation, and when it happens, every special-interest group in the world comes out of the woodwork to get a piece of the pie.

Skipping all the gory details, in a few hours, we had outlined a process to get things done in three years, and an abbreviated process which condensed consultation and created a parallel track for writing the legislation during the consultative process.

I reassured them that I knew the project couldn't be done and then got agreement around the following principle: "let's get started based on what we have done here and move forward as quickly as we can."

When we get to the point of impossibility or where something can't happen, you tell me exactly what the problem is and what's required to solve it. I will go to the Minister of Energy and tell him why we aren't going to get it done.

Then he can choose whether or not to postpone the project, get us extra resources or do whatever is required to solve the problem, if possible."

We arranged an intense schedule of meetings and consultations. At every meeting, I reminded them that I knew that we couldn't accomplish the task but that we were going to go at it as hard as we could until we hit the big "impossible" stop sign.

You know the end of the story. We got it done against all odds. The bill passed that legislative session. Another victory for The Results Equation.

Chapter 32

What Kind of Projects Need the Results Equation™ ?

In Chapter 31 I gave a small sample of projects where the equation process has been applied successfully. That is by no means a complete list, but it demonstrates the scope of possibilities.

Some straightforward projects that are easy to conceptualize and involve limited time and processes may not need any help at all. It would be a waste of time to create some formal process to tie your shoes.

You already know what feels like to have a project where you know exactly what to do, have the interest and drive to get it done and know when you'll make time to do it.

Answering the question "What kinds of projects?" is more about defining the characteristic of the project than any particular discipline or area of work.

Projects you have put off repeatedly. Projects you have started and stopped multiple times. Projects that have been in the corporate plan for two or three years but never seem to get done.

Projects that involve a lot of personal reflection and change. Projects that you know you "should" do but keep finding reasons to put off. Projects that scare you. Projects with many parts. Projects with high conflict potential.

What about a project that intimidates you? A project like this is an ideal candidate. It may be because you don't know what you don't know. You may not know how long it will take and can't see a way to figure that out.

You may not know how to get the support you think you need to make the project happen, either in the company or your family. You may not be able to articulate what you want, but you know something needs to happen.

You have a ridiculous deadline. There is significant opposition either in your own heart or from others who might be affected or associated with the project.

The Results Equation shines brightest when projects seem daunting, and you feel overwhelmed right out of the gate.

When the commitment is high to get something done, the equation will be the catalyst to get your project over the goal line. There is no category of project that won't work, and there is no industry or vertical where the principles and processes will not apply.

Doing an in-depth gut check with the five questions and the six principles discussed in earlier chapters will tell you whether you are ready to use the results equation process.

Chapter 33

Big Projects or Small Projects

There is a saying "One man's trash is another man's treasure." What seems like a scary project to one person may be easy for someone else. The size of the project is not the issue.

Some projects take several years, require long and detailed planning across multiple disciplines, considerable budgets, and a large staff.

Other projects are private and involve one or perhaps two people. Projects like this can be just as difficult and intense because of the nature of the changes involved.

A better way to think about this is not "big or small," but "easy or difficult." This is particularly true when you have an objective that has been on your radar for a long time.

If you have repeatedly tried to change something in your life and have failed, there's a reason. The results equation will help you identify the reason and make a conscious choice about whether you dare to make the changes.

The equation is particularly effective when you are trying to add something new to an already full life. For example, perhaps you want to start a business.

You likely don't have a great deal of empty time to fill if you're already leading a productive and full life. You may be driven to do something more and wondering how to find the time.

You may have a yearning to start a business that reflects a talent or skill that you have. You might believe you have no idea how to create products and services and market them effectively, mainly because you're already working a regular job or you've never done anything like that before.

You may have relationship challenges that are hindering personal growth and have no idea how to go about addressing them even though they have been bothering you for years.

Because the equation process includes internal mindset, personal habits and other "soft" areas that are often overlooked in planning and execution programs, it's capable of handling even the thorniest situations.

More importantly than listing all kinds of projects that might benefit from the equation, perhaps you're reflecting right this minute on some things you want to do in your personal or corporate life that has stubbornly eluded you.

If you are wondering if this system is up to your challenge, the answer is an emphatic yes. You will be best served by beginning now. Figure out how to apply the results equation to create the new reality you're longing.

Another trap is spending time trying to figure out why the equation won't work for your particular challenge. It will. Spending time finding reasons not to move forward is an indication of how deeply we're stuck in a rut.

Chapter 34

Extra Cheese

When I order pizza, I'm a big fan of extra cheese. There's something innately satisfying about the thick strands of cheese stretching as I pull out the first slice.

I use the analogy of extra cheese when people ask: "How deep do I use the results equation?" In other words, for best results, how deeply do I need to dive into the problem?

The best answer is always the simplest. When you use the equation, you create several documents that guide you in making changes and creating the results you want.

When you get finished with the documents, if they don't inspire you with absolute confidence and provide you with a clear roadmap to success, you have not gone deep enough.

On the other hand, if you find yourself getting bogged down in endless detail because of some need for "perfectionism and certainty," then you've gone too deep and allowed the process itself to become a hindrance.

The equation process is a roadmap to freedom. When applied correctly it gives hope and light to every situation almost before the work begins.

That is how you can tell whether you are effectively applying the process. With documents in hand and introspection done at the right depth, you feel clear, empowered and certain about your ability to create the result you desire.

It takes practice and some iteration to get this right, but the more you treat the process as a friend instead of a burden, the better it performs for you.

Ultimately, the results equation is a voyage of discovery and liberation. If it feels like wandering around in the dark, then start over and figure out where you went off the path.

The equation is based on the truth that you *can* create the results you want in your life. You created the ones you have. You will produce your future results. Why not make them the ones you want?

The big question is whether you want to create a future on purpose or whether you want to aimlessly flow down the river with the raft you're on.

Your future is in your hands. You can create any result you want. This is true in your personal life, in your business, in your relationships and every piece of your existence.

Taking control and creating the results you want is the opportunity the equation puts squarely in your hands. It's a powerful tool and will be your best friend if you choose.

The equation process is not a band-aid to create temporary fixes for long-standing problems. It's not just a vocabulary to create words that build no momentum. It is certainly not a "flavor of the month," process to be tried and discarded because "it didn't work."

It is the most powerful goal achievement system I have seen. Properly applied it will carry your raft to any shore you want.

In the following chapters, I give examples of how the equation has been applied to achieve the type of goals and create the kind of personal change I'm talking about.

Chapter 35

Writing Books

One study said 85% of adults believe they should write a book. Something about their life experience, or things they have seen or learned makes them feel that they have something important to say.

Less than one percent write that book. As a result, we never find out what happened to them to make them feel like they had important wisdom to share with us.

Depending on the statistics you read, between 1,000 and 3,000 books are published everyday. While that may present the authors with a marketing challenge in terms of getting an audience and selling their book, it's sad that only one percent actually write that book.

As an author of many books and a coach whose mission it is to help people do things they don't believe they can do, the equation is a perfect fit to help those who want to write a book, create a course or, like my present creative project, finish two albums of original music.

Most people who want to write a book are not authors, per se. They have jobs, or they run a business, and their lives are already full. The thought of writing a book is so overwhelming and daunting that they never start.

Some of the big questions that come up are:

- Am I good enough writer?
- What if I write it and it flops?
- Even if I write it, how do I get it published?
- Do I have anything to say?
- Will anybody want to read it?
- Isn't what I want to write already said somewhere?
- Am I important enough to get noticed?
- How do I get started?
- And many similar questions.

Using the results equation to write my first few books proved the power of the process. It helped collect and organize my thinking, fit the work in my busy schedule, create a deadline, produce a good book, get it published and sold and achieve bestseller status on Amazon.

Later in my coaching practice, it became evident that many clients, regardless of their existing job or business, also wanted to write a book.

Some wanted to write it to help their marketing. Some wanted to write it to clarify their message or get their message out to a wider audience. Others wanted it to help create products and services.

Regardless of the reason, the barriers and challenges were the same – having enough time, organizing and expressing the material coherently and keeping motivation up to get to the end of the project.

Remember the four questions:

- Where are you?
- Where do you want to go?
- What is the path?
- How do you keep moving?

In this case, the answers to the first two questions are easy. Where am I? I don't have a book now. Where do I want to be? I want to have a book finished, published and available to the public in one year.

The real focus for this problem is on questions #3 and #4. What's of particular importance is the part of the equation that deals with courageous planning.

Mapping all the steps required, estimating the time needed and most importantly, fitting the work into a life already full of other things are the critical keys to getting it done.

After that, creating the courage and energy to keep moving is the remaining ingredient to get the project over the goal line.

Now, many clients and successful books later, this process has proved to be the fastest, easiest and most powerful way to get this done.

After many iterations, I have also created other aids specifically aimed at writing books or creating courses. The Story Arc™ framework is an organizing principle that helps authors and content creators get clear about messaging, focus and their intended outcome.

The Story Arc™ meshes completely with The Results Equation™ because it makes "creating the future" a snap. When you've completed the story arc, you have a powerful vision and know exactly what you want your publication to achieve.

Chapter 36

Creating Businesses

Creating businesses is another natural fit for the Results Equation. Anyone building a business likely already has a job and a full life.

Finding time to turn the side-hustle into a profitable business, usually with the idea of stepping out of the rat race and being an entrepreneur, is a big dream for many people.

The problem is that no one ever really knows how hard this is. If you haven't attempted this, you can't have a sense of all the pieces involved and how much time and effort it takes.

Starting with the end in mind, one of the principles from the legendary book *Seven Habits of Highly Effective People* is an essential launch point for creating a business.

As obvious as that is, I am constantly amazed by people that want to create a business and can't describe a specific future vision. What exactly are you going to sell? Who, exactly, is going to buy it? Why will they pay for it?

How will you produce this product? How will you market it and get it in front of those who need it? How will you find time to do any of this given that your life is full?

Most people come with an astounding lack of clarity. It's not weird to have a great idea without knowing how to make it happen. Resistance to getting clear about the intent, benefit, target market, pricing and other elements essential to a successful product launch spells failure.

Creating time in the schedule, getting buy-in from a spouse or family members and managing a business growth process while balancing a full life are all dismissed with a hopeful "I just know I have to do this."

The equation process is a precise and specific way to map out where you want to go, exactly what it takes to get there, how long this will take and how you intend to fit it into your current busy life.

The four questions are paramount.

1 Where are you now? Usually, the answer is, "I have an idea, but not a business."

2. Where do you want to go? After some work, the answer to this question is usually "I want to be in business full-time selling a range of products and services based around this idea."

After more work, we have specifics around the product, the market, the marketing, the effort and time required to create the product or service and all the rest.

3. What is the path? This is where it gets thorny. If you have a busy life now, you have to make explicit trades. You have to be willing to give up certain things you are doing now to find time to create the new business or project. Usually, we just think we can "cram it in" somewhere.

That rarely happens, and so most businesses never get started. If they do, there isn't enough time or saved money to get them off the ground, and they become one of the casualties in the studies that say that 85% of new businesses fail within the first five years.

4. How do you keep moving? Usually, this is a vague assertion that the current desire will maintain motivation. The fact that this feels weak as we discuss this demonstrates that this is inadequate.

Without a specific process to maintain internal motivation and manage external critical path steps, the vision is destined to remain only a vision. With these processes in place, the new business has a real chance.

The section of the equation that requires clear mapping of the steps, time and money involved is the essential ingredient.

The results equation shines by requiring you to explicitly make trades in your calendar so you can tell what it takes to complete the project you've told yourself you want.

After many successful business launches and product creation processes, I have seen the equation in action and know without a doubt it is the most powerful and effective way to make this dream come true.

Do you have an idea you want to turn into a product or service? Do you have a dream about exiting the rat race and launching a career on your terms?

If you do, the equation is the answer.

Chapter 37

Mending Fences

Moving away from concrete and tangible examples to more "touchy-feely" areas, let's talk about work in the murky area of relationships.

All of us have relationships which have been damaged by our own or others' actions. We know they are in need or repair. Often these situations languish for years, and one or both parties ache to make some kind of changes but have no idea what to do or how to start.

Consequently, these situations don't get resolved. They perpetually linger until people die or a significant external change forces the parties to be face-to-face and have the hard conversations necessary to start on the path to healing.

Even then, there may be no real resolution. People stumble through funerals, estate disposition and other required but temporary processes and return sulking to previous grievances.

Why wait? Why allow externalities to dictate when and how these situations get resolved? Why not take ownership of the situation, regardless of who was "at fault" and be the one who makes the first move?

Because the Results Equation deals explicitly with issues of self-love, self-esteem, forgiveness, and the difficult internal areas that are often the barriers to reconciliation, it's the ideal way to take ownership and create positive movement.

One of the most challenging things associated with relationship repair is blaming. Grudges live for so long because we're fixated on the desire to have someone else apologize and acknowledge their responsibility.

The equation process focuses on honesty. Part of honesty is assessing your willingness to fix the relationship regardless of others' behaviors or actions.

If your desire to repair the relationship exists only "if so-and-so apologizes for such and such," you're not ready. You can start with the Understanding the Present and the Mental Earthquake parts of the equation to see what you can create in your own heart before proceeding.

Assessing blame and exacting punishment is not consistent with self-analysis and self-control. No matter what your current view of the situation, it always takes two to tango and every relationship problem has two sides.

A choice to be honest and accept your responsibility might be a great starting point and a way to find an opening to begin the repair. Also, the emphasis on self-love will create an awareness in you that might bring you to a more liberal and forgiving viewpoint.

Perhaps it's not even necessary to receive the apology you have so deeply longed for. What if you expand your circle of love to the point where it supersedes all bitterness and anger?

One fundamental discovery in the equation is that it's impossible to control the feelings, thoughts or behavior of another. Continually hanging your success and state of mind on what someone else thinks and feels is a recipe for disaster.

As you take responsibility for your own thoughts and feelings and choose to live from a place of love and self-determination, your view on the repair needed and the actions required will change dramatically.

I have seen the equation repair "intractable and unsolvable" dilemmas and create deep and meaningful conversations and love where none existed before.

Because the Results Equation deals with the "softer" issues of personal attitudes and behaviors, it can succeed where nothing else seems to make a dent.

Chapter 38

Creating Personal Change

Most personal development systems treat personal change as a simple matter of creating new habits. The truth is much deeper and far more inclusive.

You created the life you have now with your current behaviors and attitudes. Until those fundamental beliefs and attitudes change, you will continue to create the energy and the outcomes you have right now.

The Results Equation is extraordinarily adept at delving into the deepest areas of thought and exploring the connections between thoughts, feelings, and behavior.

We often stop making progress toward a goal because "we don't feel like it." What if "feeling like it" has nothing to do with how you perform? What if how you feel is entirely under your control?

Discovering that you are the architect of your present reality is a profound and life-altering shift that you can make and use to your advantage by applying the equation process.

The downfall of many attempts at personal change lies partly in the labels and language we use. When we use labels to describe ourselves as "being" a certain way, we limit our opportunities.

For example, "I'm disorganized," "I'm not a detail person," or "I've always been this way." A hundred labels like these are disempowering and sit at the core of our excuses to underperform and miss out on our divine potential.

When we consistently apply labels to ourselves, we reinforce a "truth" that is a lie. This is not to say you didn't behave consistently with that description. Maybe you did – in the past. That was *then*; this is *now*.

This doesn't mean you will *always* behave that way, or you *must* behave that way, or you're *genetically predisposed* to behave that way. It doesn't even mean you will behave that way *one* more time.

As with most things, the beginning of change lies with a willingness to tell the truth. Are you willing to be honest with yourself about what you think and feel? Combined with the master key of taking responsibility, honesty is the first step.

What happens when you look in the mirror and say, "I love you?" In your private moments, how do you talk about yourself? Are you willing to entertain the idea that your ability to love others is limited by your ability to love yourself? Are you willing to explore the possibility that your growth potential is unlimited if you pursue it?

One difficulty with personal change is our desire to do everything at once. We may have a list of things we want to fix immediately – and, we wanted the results yesterday.

Sometimes it seems like this is "just how the world should work." After all, everything else seems to be solvable in the length of a TV sitcom episode.

Real growth is not like this at all. Every aspect of growth and change requires a process, appropriate support and time.

Wherever you put your time, love and attention, you will create growth. If you're willing to turn your time, love and attention to yourself, you can create anything you want in any part of your life.

The equation process digs deep and lets you come face-to-face with who you are and whom you want to be. You also create a precious opportunity to make choices about what you want in a neutral and safe place.

That's not to say that we do psychotherapy in this process. We don't. Psychologists and psychiatrists typically focus on taking something that is broken and fixing it.

Coaching, along with the Results Equation focuses on taking someone who is relatively healthy but stuck in their own thoughts, feelings, and stories and helping them create a new context and infinite possibility.

If you're willing to start with the truth, stay with the truth and persevere in keeping commitments, nothing is outside your reach.

Chapter 39

Managing Corporate Change

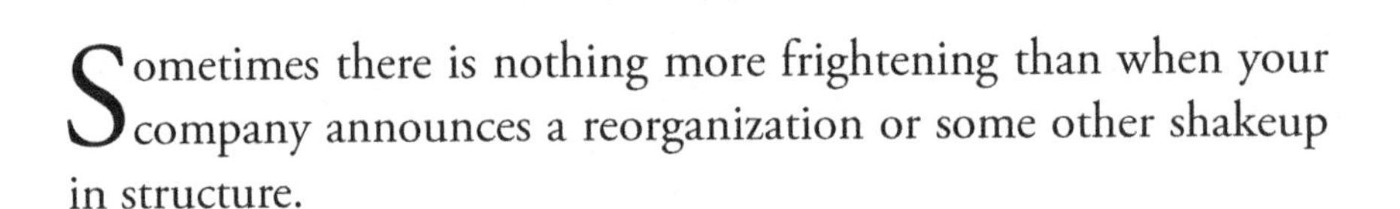

Sometimes there is nothing more frightening than when your company announces a reorganization or some other shakeup in structure.

Fear runs rampant; rumors spread like wildfire and everybody starts to look for the evil demon hidden behind the watercooler.

Like everything else, change in the corporate structure is often needed, healthy and exciting. I have used the equation process to manage several such corporate change processes.

As with everything else, the founding principle is honesty. It is a fundamental fact that people and organizations take their cue from leadership.

If leaders are lethargic, unenthusiastic, pessimistic and seem like they're hiding something, then everyone in every department will be convinced that something terrible is about to happen. Often, they believe they won't know what's coming until it's too late to do anything.

Firmly committing to the three choices in Chapters 20, 21 and 22 and modeling the six principles in Chapter 23 is vital and must start before organization changes are planned.

Clear outcome objectives and decisions about processes and communication commitments are essential starting points to move successfully through the process.

Even though different goal types require a different emphasis on each of the equation's five parts, nothing can be omitted. As you read in Chapter 30 on Relentless Execution, apply the principle "Execute, Evaluate, Adjust."

In a corporate reorganization, this principle is critical. It's an inevitable fact that unintended consequences and new information will surface during the process. It must be clear that evaluation and adjustment are expected and not signs of uncertainty or error.

A regular review process, comparison to original objectives and continuing commitment to open communication is critical during these changes.

In Chapter 26, "Understanding the Present," the questions about "where are we now?" and "how did we get here?" are important to discuss and share with those potentially affected by the change.

Cooperation and buy-in are fostered by openness, communication and a clear understanding of the starting point, endpoint and the timeframe.

The learning that comes from Understanding the Present must be clear and present for everyone, not just the leadership instituting the change.

If the objective of the change is clear and the benefits demonstrable, then the next question "why are we not moving?" can and should be framed so everyone understands the barriers in the current structure and process, and can buy into the need for adjustment.

Every term in the results equation creates a lexicon which, when properly implemented, enhances communication. The specific words can change, but the principle of creating a common language around the starting point, path, and the objectives creates internal unity and momentum.

Regardless of careful planning and communication, there will always be someone or some group of people who choose not to understand, choose to rebel, choose not to participate and perhaps choose to be obstructionist.

This is not uncommon and should be expected. Part of the "Courageous Plan" created in Chapter 29 must include a process to deal with bumps in the road. Some of the bumps may be unexpected outcomes, and some may be unsupportive reactions.

Obstacles and setbacks are normal processes in any change effort. The attitude and actions to deal with obstacles, be they personnel problems or unexpected discoveries, should be a part of the plan right from the beginning.

Often change processes are iterative and successive movements are required to achieve the objective. I'm not suggesting multiple reorganizations; I am suggesting multiple evaluations of progress during the reorganization implementation.

A final factor is the ability of leadership to be honest and forthright if circumstances dictate a variation from the initial plan. The reasons and timeframe for adjustments must be communicated, and if mistakes were made, those need to be openly admitted and discussed.

Nothing is more damaging to change than the feeling of secrecy. If somebody is hiding something to save face or because they don't know the answer, it undermines everything. It's far better to say "I'm not sure," than to pretend otherwise.

Chapter 40

Leadership and Corporate Culture

Sometimes corporate changes involve less structural work and more work on changing its culture.

Over the last several decades, there have been all kinds of cultural revolutions in the workplace. All are designed to improve productivity, dedication, and commitment. Some are also a reflection of changing sensitivities to important cultural issues of diversity, fairness, and inclusion.

This was particularly important after the economic downturns in the 1980s when corporate largesse to employees vanished forever and many experienced employment upheavals that were unexpected and traumatic.

This spawned an attitude that continues today. Many employees have little loyalty, a suspicious outlook and short-term expectations, which is problematic for corporations who depend on people.

The upheaval of the recent past and the global market of today teach workers that they can't depend on their corporations when the bottom line is at stake. We need a new equilibrium based on value creation, communication, and cooperation.

Corporate culture comes directly from leadership. If you want to affect the culture of an organization, it must start at the top. That doesn't necessarily mean every change needs to start with the CEO, but it must start with the leader of the affected area.

It's frequently true that one department has had a leader with a style that creates suspicion, negativity, poor communication, and other problems.

Regardless of the scope of the change, department-wide or corporate-wide, the key is that the leader shapes the culture. The leader needs to articulate and visibly model the culture with integrity before it begins to be believable.

Consequently, corporate culture change is not a program, a slogan, vision statements on the wall or any other gimmick. It's not to say that such goals and visions aren't necessary. It is to say that before they're effective, the leader must articulate and demonstrate the values in every transaction.

The leader likely needs to look inward and move through personal change processes before they begin to talk openly about changing the culture of the department or organization.

As I noted in Chapter 38 on personal change, honesty is the biggest barrier here. Most leaders can't see what they're doing wrong, much less admit failings that are creating the problems they want to eliminate.

Because of this blind spot, problems fester until they explode. The resulting culture change is then mandated from the outside, from emerging conflict or problems that show up in the bottom line.

When outside forces are the impetus for change; it creates another problem. These events often create an atmosphere of panic which is not conducive to culture change.

The bottom line is this: whether the transformation is imposed from without or chosen by an introspective visionary leader, it must be driven by that leader.

A coach working with the leader, helping them discover currently underdeveloped personal characteristics, blind spots and counterproductive behaviors that are required, is usually the first step to effective culture change.

Coaching may last a few months or longer depending on the "coachability" of the leader, the commitment to the change and the skill of the coach.

After the leader becomes comfortable being the model of the new culture, it's appropriate to describe behaviors that need changing throughout the organization.

To summarize; corporate culture starts at the top. The leader must personally understand, support and model the desired attributes, behaviors, communication style and openness they are seeking to engender.

The leader will likely need to go through some personal work to begin those changes before they're accepted and effective in the organization.

This is best done before disaster hits so that the additional stress of business performance, blaming and fear isn't a part of the process.

When a disaster has already occurred, then a major intervention is required. The CEO, executive leadership team and others need to be intensely involved in personal change, or nothing will save the organization.

The Results Equation is perfectly suited for this type of significant intervention. However, application by a skilled coach and committed leadership team is essential for success.

When leadership changes are firmly in place, there is high probability of success in creating the desired culture within the organization.

Chapter 41

Results Equation Lifestyle

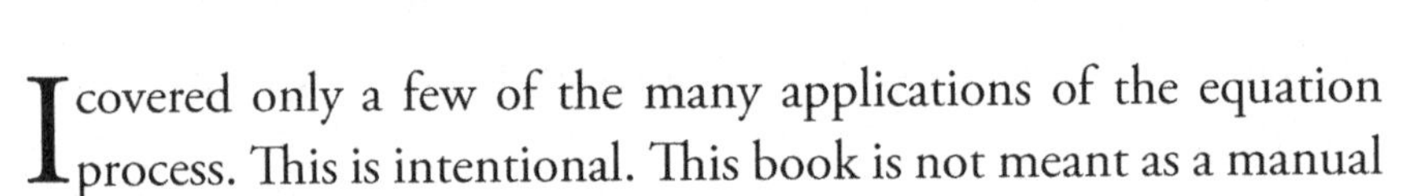

I covered only a few of the many applications of the equation process. This is intentional. This book is not meant as a manual to apply this tool to a particular situation.

Rather, it's an explanation of how it works, and a guide to spark thinking about how this flexible yet intense process can be applied to any situation.

Every problem is unique. While high-level outcomes are simple to state, when you consider the people involved, the circumstances leading to the problem, the exact situation to change and the goal to achieve, it wouldn't be useful to try to be prescriptive and specific with examples of application.

The examples spanning both personal and corporate processes should give you the sense that the applications are broad and varied and there is no situation where the questions, principles, and steps of the equation process cannot produce the result you want.

I call this chapter "Results Equation Lifestyle," because the principles articulated in the equation have become a way of life for many clients that I have helped and, of course, myself.

It's founded on the idea that a mindset of "Choice, Ownership, and Possibility" creates opportunity and success. This mindset combined with the choices in Chapters 20, 21 and 22 and the principles in Chapter 23, create an unshakable foundation for success with the equation.

This's not to say that *every decision* takes analysis and walking through the specific steps. It is to say that a choice to live the principles of the equation is a framework from which you can create a productive and influential life.

Adopting a commitment of rigorous honesty, where you look in the mirror and always tell the truth is immensely liberating. Every decision is without ulterior motive and everyone around you knows that what you say is what you mean and what they see is what they get.

With a life founded in honesty and transparency, intuition is clear, decisions are faster and more accurate, and you carry no baggage.

Understanding your motivations or desires is another significant key in living a lifestyle that's productive and unfettered by internal conflicts.

The ability to express what you want in clear and unambiguous terms serves as an anchor and guidepost to create decision frameworks for anything that comes in your path.

If you do more in-depth work and connect the desires you have to the purpose you feel in life; you are in the enviable position of alignment where your life purpose, your work, and all your decisions focus in the same direction.

Based on implementing the first two principles in Chapter 23, the principle of imagination is then enhanced to a degree only enjoyed by those who are in alignment. Imagination is the root of all advancement. "Genius is one percent inspiration, and 99% perspiration," is a quote credited to Einstein.

Both parts are critical. Without 1% inspiration or imagination, the 99% perspiration would just be a lot of sweat. Without the relentless execution described by the 99% perspiration then 1% imagination is simply an empty dream.

Intuition, imagination, inspiration or whatever you choose to call it functions more clearly in a framework of rigorous honesty and clarity of desire.

The fourth principle to guide your results equation lifestyle is optimism. As I mentioned earlier, optimistic people live longer, make more money, are happier, perform better on the sports field and in the board room and generally have a lot more fun.

When you live believing that things are possible, you are much more likely to see potential solutions instead of intractable problems.

My experience in troubleshooting and doing difficult assignments for many years has indisputably demonstrated this truth over and over again.

Optimism is a choice. If you currently hold a pessimistic stance toward life, the equation process is the perfect vehicle for you to begin personal change and become a different person. The rewards are fantastic.

If you choose to live a lifestyle based on the principle of determination, it should be evident that you'll get more done. If you're determined to create an outcome despite opposition and in the face of any challenge, you develop an attitude of "I can do this."

That attitude is the attitude of leadership. People flock to follow the leader who is confident and clear about the direction they are going. If leadership and accomplishment are things you want, then determination is an indispensable ingredient.

Sometimes people confuse humility with being a doormat. Nothing could be further from the truth.

For our purposes, here are three points of emphasis.

- First, humility is the characteristic that allows you to learn from anyone whether they drive a Bentley or push a shopping cart.
- Second, humility is the determination to look for the gift in every setback rather than complain to the establishment or at God because trouble has crossed your path.
- Third, humility is the willingness to let others' light shine brightly and get credit. It's the banishment of ego driven by selfishness and the need for acclaim.

One great quote is "A lot can get done when no one cares who gets the credit." Countless projects have been derailed and long-standing animosity fostered by the battle over who gets the glory.

The Results Equation is about making things happen, particularly difficult things. It's based on the most profound internal truths and the most powerful principles of love, truth, good planning, and execution.

It will work for you in creating personal change and advancing the work you want to do in the world. It starts with a commitment in your heart to be the person you can be.

That singular commitment will do more to ensure your success in the long run than any other thing you can begin. The challenge for you is to decide whether you want to take responsibility and use the equation to grow.

Those that embrace it create enormous success. They do it with calmness, certainty, and joy. Your opportunity is to start now to figure out ways to apply the equation process to the most complicated and challenging problems you currently face.

Remember, it always starts with you.

Chapter 42

Getting Help

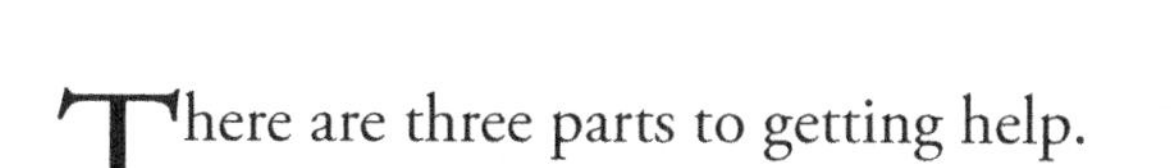

There are three parts to getting help.

- First, recognize that help is right for you and is available.
- Second, be willing to spend the time, energy and cash it takes to find and retain help.
- Third, be willing to accept coaching and be coached.

Recognizing the need to get help is complicated. For some reason, we think we should be able to do everything ourselves. We view asking for or needing help as a sign of failure or weakness.

This is false since no athlete ever reached the heights of state, regional, national or Olympic fame without one or more coaches in their corner.

Why would we assume that actors, athletes, musicians and performers who work and perform at the highest level need coaches, yet we, who are trying to make the most of ourselves and create tremendous achievements, are somehow supposed to do everything alone?

When we look at it this way, perhaps the notion of getting help is less offensive. Below are some questions that'll show how having help or a coach will get you to your desired results faster and easier.

Can you get to your goal faster with help than without it?

Does your intuition tell you that outside perspective, accountability, and other tools that come from getting help will result in greater achievements?

If you change the paradigm from "I need help" to "I'll get there faster if I have someone helping me along the way," then getting help moves you from weakness to a smart choice.

The truth is, you might be able to get there alone. It will take longer, be more difficult and you'll be more prone to quit or fail than if you get help. The real question is "Why on earth would you do it the slow way on purpose?"

In my work as a coach, it's always the case that if you want to get to the goal line, getting the right help makes it easier and faster.

Second is being willing to spend the time, energy and cash it takes to retain a coach. If you haven't used a coach before, you might feel like getting a coach is a crap shoot. It might seem like you're throwing money away, hoping something good will happen.

The process of finding and retaining a coach takes some education and work. Talk to a couple of coaches, see how the conversation feels. If the conversation is just about how good they are and how many people they've helped, look elsewhere.

On the other hand, if you feel lighter, freer and more creative, that's a good start. Furthermore, if you start to believe in yourself and the doubts seem less dark and the fears less intimidating, you might be in the right place.

At the end of the day, hiring a coach that's a good fit for your temperament and helps you feel like the possibilities are real and within your grasp, can be the single most effective thing to get you moving. That goes double for a difficult project.

Good coaching is not free, nor is it cheap. If you're looking for bargain-basement coaches, then there are many schools that produce them, and there are many to choose from. Don't settle for the bargain-basement school of achievement.

If an athlete wants to reach their highest performance, they look for the coach that will inspire them to get to that level of competence. They look for the power, not to the pocketbook. Coaching will pay for itself at least ten times over if you find a good one and you're prepared to go all in.

That leads us to part three – your willingness to be coached. My experience is that 90% of people I talk to at any given time, are not ready to be coached.

That doesn't mean they don't want things. It just means they aren't ready for the rigors of self-examination and accountability. At this moment they aren't willing to do the work of growth.

Reading a book and watching YouTube videos is not coaching. While entertaining and able to provide you with many insights and "aha" moments, without follow-up coaching, they will evaporate like the morning dew.

I recently had a conversation with a prospect who told me they went to a month-long, high-powered and expensive program. During the program, accountability was high, motivation was high, and everything felt successful.

When they finished the program, "real life" came back into play. There was no further accountability. Behavioral and other belief changes weren't anchored deeply enough, so everything slid back to normal, including the frustration of not having successful change.

Creating sustained actions needed to live a life fueled by truth and the principles of the Results Equation takes time. You need to be prepared to invest personal effort and energy and do the "personal development push-ups."

No one believes an athlete gets to the top of their sport without many hours spent practicing. Yet somehow, we think that if we read books, listen to speeches and watch videos that we will make personal changes.

Personal change requires "personal development push-ups." The exercise and continued application of principles, aided by an external eye and your willingness to make change happen, are all essential ingredients.

That said, with a coach that is suited to your desires and needs, making these changes is not only doable but enjoyable. Creating a lifestyle of results and an eye tuned to new habits and beliefs is fun and rewarding.

The best and fastest route to creating the result you want is to get a coach. If you would like to have a conversation with me about the possibility of working through one of my programs, my contact information is in the Appendix.

Whether or not you opt for participation in one of my programs or get help in another fashion, the key will be to accept and implement the three parts of getting help at the start of this chapter.

Help is essential if you want rapid and permanent progress. Be willing to invest the time, energy and cash required to find and retain a good coach. Expect to work with them at least a year.

Look into your heart and decide whether you are prepared for the adventure of coaching and creating a new version of yourself that is keen and capable of getting to any achievement you can imagine.

Epilogue

Eleven years on, the work I described in the prologue is still in place. The legislation was sound; the regulatory body created was accepted and is performing its functions for the province very well.

The political landscape has changed; priorities have moved away from those that drove the fire drill of the day. New priorities and urgent problems have come to replace the old.

The beautiful thing is that the Results Equation worked then and works now. In the last two years, I have conducted over 30 workshops teaching and coaching. The workshops last 90 days and help those who participate in creating a big goal.

The workshops have been incredibly successful and have proven repeatedly, that the equation is a powerful framework and tool to make things happen.

However, for you, all the things that I've done with the equation process don't matter. What objectives are in your mind right now?

What personal changes do you want to make that would make your life better and more fulfilling?

What business improvement or growth is nagging at you yet remains unaccomplished? What corporate change opportunities lay before you that you're not doing because you don't know how?

The equation will only matter to you if you pick some significant change or project and then rigorously apply this to prove to yourself that you can get it done.

As a coach, most of all I love the feeling that comes when a client realizes that they already possess the skills and talents to create a life they want. It is possible!

Suddenly, they begin to remove barriers. If there is fear, procrastination, and self-sabotage that may have been holding them back for years or even decades, they begins to lose their grip.

When change begins to happen, new energy and new life flow into a person. Over and over again the experience of joyful discovery and mindful creation is an exciting process that I never stop enjoying.

If you already accomplish everything you set out to do, then you have a system that works for you. If, like most people, you dream and then don't complete things, look deep in your soul and decide what it's worth to you to change the story.

What would it take for you to become a person who does what they say they're going to do? What satisfaction would come by learning the skills to make things happen according to your plans and deepest desires?

Don't delay your opportunities and fulfillment any longer. For help, see the contact information in the Appendix. Start today. Use the Results Equation™ to create what you want in your life. Now!

Appendix and Contact Information

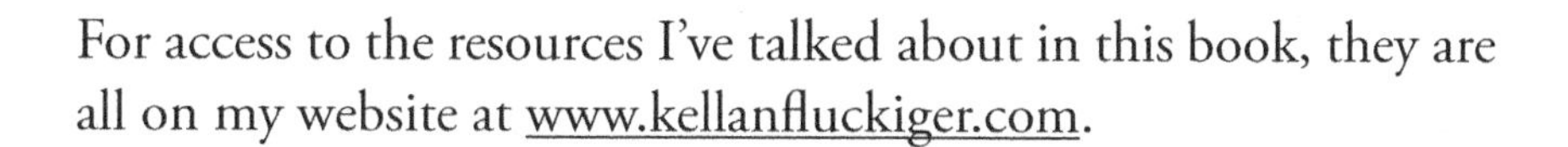

For access to the resources I've talked about in this book, they are all on my website at www.kellanfluckiger.com.

- *The Book of Context* and *Meeting God at the door* are available in paperback, Audible and digital (Kindle). If you order it from my website, you'll receive a signed copy. Otherwise, it's available on Amazon.com and Amazon.ca.

- Meditation Books – Volume I in my 5-part series is *Meditation, The Amazing Journey Within.* Four additional volumes on meditation will be available in paperback, Kindle, and Audible.

- Meditation music – there are many apps available for smartphones. I wrote a piece called Inner Sanctum: Circles of Peace. A sample of this music is available for free on my website.

Information on creating effective and powerful morning rituals including Spiritual, Physical, Emotional, and Mental components, and especially the powerful self-love components is part of my Results Equation Intentive program. More information is available at www.resultsequationintensive.com.

To learn more about coaching and the work I do with individual and corporate clients, you will need to provide your name, email address and phone number before booking an appointment at www.kellanfluckiger.com.

I frequently use social media as a platform to discuss everything in this book and other coaching processes that I use. Follow me on Facebook at www.facebook.com/kellan.fluckiger3 and on Twitter @kellanfluckiger.

I've created a number of free video series to help you get unstuck, stop procrastinating, end self-sabotage and get you moving on your way to success, prosperity, and happiness. You'll find them on my YouTube channel – Ultimate Life Formula. To keep up with everything that's going on and get the latest video series, it's best to subscribe to my channel.

About the Author

Kellan Fluckiger is the author of the #1 best-selling books *TightRope of Depression* and *Meeting God at the Door*, an in-demand speaker, and highly successful coach. Working with CEOs of companies large and small, Kellan has transformed and touched many lives over the past 30 years.

A certified master coach and former C-suite Executive, Kellan has coached everyone from Super Bowl winners to BMI Award Winners and everyone in between.

Kellan is a master at high achievement. As a motivational speaker and business coach, his journey has benefited thousands. He has written five books on meditation and provides coaching and support for creative's, entrepreneurs and leaders on their journey through struggles and victories as they discover, develop and deliver their talents to the world.

In addition to coaching, Kellan has written, recorded and produced 11 albums of original music. He's been running a successful recording studio for over 35 years. Samples of Kellan's music are available on his website at www.kellanfluckiger.com.

Born in San Francisco, Kellan now spends most of the year creating and writing in Canada with his wife, Joy and their 2 cats and 2 dogs.

Made in the USA
Middletown, DE
26 May 2019